A
PLATOON LEADER'S
TOUR

A PLATOON LEADER'S TOUR

AS TOLD BY
U.S. ARMY PLATOON LEADERS

CENTER FOR THE ADVANCEMENT OF LEADER
DEVELOPMENT & ORGANIZATIONAL LEARNING
WEST POINT, NEW YORK

authorHOUSE®

AuthorHouse™
1663 Liberty Drive
Bloomington, IN 47403
www.authorhouse.com
Phone: 1-800-839-8640

Published by AuthorHouse   12/20/2012

ISBN: 978-1-4772-9944-9 (sc)
ISBN: 978-1-4772-9942-5 (hc)
ISBN: 978-1-4772-9943-2 (e)

Library of Congress Control Numver: 2012923818

This book is printed on acid-free paper.

This book should be cited as:

Platoon Leaders. A Platoon Leader's Tour. West Point, NY: Center for the Advancement of Leader Development & Organizational Learning, 2010.

To contact the editors, email PL.team@us.army.mil.

The Army Study Program and the Army Research Institute provided resources for the development and distribution of this book.

i

Cover art by Guy Rogers III.

CONTENTS

A Platoon Leader's Tour

PREFACE

The stories in this book are told <u>by</u> and <u>for</u> Army platoon leaders.

We share our true stories with you because we love our country and the men and women who volunteer to defend it with their lives. Our Soldiers deserve great leadership! We hope that you will learn from our experiences and become a more effective leader, sooner. If you're like many of us, the first time you meet your platoon will be downrange, where your decisions will have life-or-death consequences.

In these pages, we don't talk much about issuing FRAGOs, executing battle drills, or formally counseling our subordinates. The schoolhouse prepares us well for those types of tasks. Instead, we use this opportunity to share some aspects of our combat deployments in Iraq that have surprised and challenged us.

Some of these stories are ones we tell only to our closest comrades. Some are told with tears streaming down our faces. Some we are proud of; others we are not. Each is true, but none is universal. Most of the time, we share our real names.

Please resist the temptation to judge us. It's easy for a future PL to imagine that she'll lead perfectly or for a past PL to forget his many mistakes. We share these stories as current PLs in combat in Iraq, where we have no such illusions.

Please accept our invitation to experience (vicariously) a tour of duty in Iraq with us as we lived it in 2006-07. Each of us has our own story, but together we tell a larger story of what it's like to be a platoon leader at war. Think of this as an extended right-seat/left-seat ride with combat-tested PLs from more than 20 battalions. Our stories are sequenced to roughly mirror a deployment, divided by month, although not every story follows from the one before it. We hope it makes sense.

The bottom line is that we will be thrilled if our stories become catalysts for conversation and professional development for all platoon leaders—past, present, and future.

It is an awesome responsibility and privilege to lead American Soldiers anytime, but especially in war. We are honored to present this collection of stories to you. May God bless you now and in the months ahead.

01 July 2010

These combat-tested platoon leaders shared their experiences in order to advance the knowledge of our profession. Although many do not have a story included in this particular book, their input impacted its development:

Clint Akins, Chris Alexander, Jesse Allgeyer, James Anderson, Dave Andros, Matthew Angoy, Eric Anthes, Craig Arnold, Andrew Artis, Randy Ashby, Travis Atwood, Nick Auletta, Casey Baker, Bernie Balsis, Dan Baringer, Mike Baskin, John Beaty, Paul Benfield, Joshua Best, Patrick Biggs, Justin Blades, Mike Blake, David Bopp, Jesse Bowman, Tommy Bramanti, Tom Broeker, Aaron Brooks, Justin Brown, Herman Bulls, Matt Burch, Jordan Burfield, Rob Burke, Sam Cartee, Greg Cartier, Stuart Chapman, Paul Charbonneau, Dan Ciccarelli, Brian Cooke, Greg Coppo, Eroch Cordts, Chris Crofford, Bryan Crossman, Jake Czekanski, Paul Daigle, Matt Dawson, Chris Dean, Chris DeFiori, Chris DeRuyter, John Dolan, Steve DuPerre, Jon Edds (RIP), Ryan Edwards, Patrick Engeman, Michael Evans, Mike Faber, Steve Ferenzi, Paddy Finnerty, Chris Ford, Jim Freeze, Tom Garvey, Keith Gauthier, Stacy Gervelis, Stephanie Gillespie, Mike Gilotti, Al Gomez, Colin Graeta, Keith Grant, Brendan Griswold, Jim Guggenheim, Mike Gunther, Neil Harber, Ryan Harbick, Brian Haas, Kai Hawkins, Pat Henson, Adam Herndon, Mike Hess, Tom Hickey, Terry Hildebrand, Pat Horan, Tucker Hughes, Brian Hurley, Mike Hutson, William Irwin, Kyle Isaacs, Bryan Jackson, Paul Janker, Pete Jodko, Phil Johnson, Mike Johnston, Shawn Jokinen, Austin Jones, Kelly Jones, Pat Kaine, Leigh Kennedy, Ed Kim, Anna King-McCrillis, Erik Klapmeier, Steve Klocko, Will Kobbe, Ryan Krackow, Bradley Krauss,

Dan Krentzman, Nick Kron, Brett Kronick, Ron Kubacki, Moonerah Lao, Brian Larson, Chris Larson, Brian Lebiednik, Jeff Ledbetter, Greg Liem, Doub Livermore, Bill Lord, Chris Lowry, Chris MacDonald, Grant MacDonald, Matthew Mackey, Dave MacPhail, Ryan Maravilla, Tina Martin, Greg Martin, Matt Martinez, John Mauro, Ben Meyer, Mike McCarty, David McCollum, Pat McGorman, Brad Mellinger, Ben Melton, Curtis Minor, Kyle Missbach, Travis Moen, Graham Morris, Billy Moss, Hector Moyano, John Moynihan, Adam Napier, Matthew Nelson, Matthew Neyland, John Nguyen, Mike Normand, Ryan Nugent, Joe Nussbaumer, Jared Oren, Aaron Pearsall, Russ Perkins, Galen Peterson, Clinton Pierce, Larry Pitts, Travis Pride, Joel Radunzel, Mike Rash, Terry Redd, Tad Reed, Neal Rice, Dan Riordan (RIP), Erich Roberts, Ted Roberts, Quinn Robertson, John Rogers, Josh Rowan, Matt Rowe, Raul Salinas, Matt Schade, Phil Schneider, Dave Shamsi, Jon Sherrill, Matthew Silva, Lee Small, Andrew Smith, Bryan Smith, Patrick Smith, Joe Snowden, David S., Clint Speegle, Morgan Spring-Glace, Mike Steele, Kevin Stein, Ryan Stidum, David Stroud, Will Sullivan, Jonathan Sweirat, Derek Syed, Tracy Tawiah, Harris Teague, John Thomas, Richard Tilly, Joe Tomasello, Travis Toole, Jeff Trinidad, Viktor Tsuber, Miguel Uc, Mike Valentine, Ben Weakley, Jeff Weaver, Laura Weimer, Thad Wescott, Jon Westbrook, Tom Whitfield, John Williams, Megan Williams, Schuyler Williamson, Alex Wilson, Wilson Winters, Dan Wise, Cecil Wolberton, Elizabeth Zerwick

PROLOGUE

Lieutenant Adam Herndon and his platoon rolled through the city streets in their up-armored Humvees. Their mission that morning was to provide convoy security to an EOD team.

"One-Six," came a report from the lead vehicle, "We have a dead body in the road."

Herndon wasn't surprised. Sectarian fighting was littering the streets of Baghdad with bodies.

"Check it out. We'll report it to the IPs," Herndon ordered.

The convoy halted. The platoon's turret-mounted gunners scanned the buildings on both sides of the street for threats. The Soldiers inside the trucks scanned the nearby curbs and street posts for any indications of an IED.

"One-Six," reported the NCO, "This guy's still alive. He's bleeding pretty bad and screaming like crazy. He's lying in the street all alone. What do you want to do?"

"Let's get a CLS out there with him and call the IPs to take him to a local hospital," replied Herndon.

The platoon and its EOD attachment maneuvered to secure the site, stopping traffic in both directions during rush hour. Horns blared as Iraqi commuters protested the inconvenience along the thoroughfare.

Herndon dismounted and moved forward along the street to the wounded man, who had been shot four times in the gut and was writhing in pain. Interspersed with prayers and moans, the panicked man explained through the interpreter that strangers had driven by and shot him with AK-47s for no apparent reason.

"I got a video camera!" yelled a squad leader. "Twelve o'clock, 300 meters, hanging out of that double-decker bus!"

Everyone knew what that meant. The only thing the insurgents valued more than killing an American was capturing the killing on video. The Soldiers took cover.

"I have a clean shot," reported the platoon's best marksman, who had immediately gotten the drop on the cameraman. The rules of engagement permitted Soldiers to kill anyone videotaping an attack.

Iraqi Army soldiers arrived, entering the platoon's perimeter over the escalating blare of horns and idling engines of the piled-up traffic. They began moving the man into the back seat of his own car so they could drive him to a hospital.

"I see a guy videotaping us," confirmed Herndon's platoon sergeant, looking through binoculars. "PID."

Herndon looked down his ACOG to positively identify the target. He saw someone leaning outside a window on the top level of the bus, looking straight back at him with a blue video camera.

"Hey, sir, can we shoot him?"

A
PLATOON LEADER'S
TOUR

MONTH ONE

1. MATT MARTINEZ

Lieutenant Matt Martinez and his wife meandered through the old German city square, admiring the gothic architecture around them.

Matt's new cell phone rang in his pocket, a ring so foreign to him he barely realized it was his.

"Hello?"

"Lieutenant Martinez, this is your company commander."

"Yes, sir."

"What are you doing? Are you far?"

"Just taking in some history, sir."

"I know I told you the other day that you weren't going to the field, but things have changed. I need you to come in. You're about to deploy."

"Roger, sir."

The newlyweds had yet to find a place to live, their car was on a boat somewhere between America and Germany, and they were still awaiting the bulk of their household goods to arrive from the States. Matt hadn't even drawn equipment from CIF.

Within two weeks, Matt was in Kuwait, preparing to go to war in Iraq.

2. JIM FREEZE

We left Kuwait about a week ago, flew to Balad Air Base, then took a helicopter flight to Camp Taji, where I currently am. In a few more days, we'll make our first drive outside of the camp to our base, FOB Warhorse. Many of us are anxious to get started making a difference, but we also have the marathon mindset that we're going to be here for 14 more months, so what's the rush?

3. GREG CARTIER

Lieutenant Greg Cartier felt someone shake his shoulder, waking him from a deep slumber. Looking up, he vaguely recognized a company commander from the BSTB.

"Come on a walk with me," the captain said.

Greg willed himself up from the cot he had collapsed onto just a few hours earlier. He and his Infantry rifle platoon had arrived in Iraq from Kuwait at 0400 that morning.

Exiting the tent, Greg's eyes were stung by the bright early-morning sun. He followed the captain across the unfamiliar dusty terrain of Camp Striker. They didn't speak.

The captain came to a halt in a motor pool. He pointed towards some large, strange vehicles.

"You see that?" he said. "That's a Buffalo. You see that?" pointing to another. "That's a Husky." Looking at Greg, he added, "I haven't trained on them either."

He escorted Greg over to a static display of various types of IEDs.

"See these? These are IEDs," he deadpanned. "This is what we're looking for."

The confusion on Greg's face must have been obvious.

"Lieutenant Cartier," the captain said, "effective immediately, your platoon is attached to my company. I just found out, too. Welcome to the Engineers. We start right-seat ride tomorrow with the route-clearance company."

"Roger, sir," Greg replied, trying to hide his frustration.

4. JIM FREEZE

Hey all,

We've been keeping very busy the last two weeks we've been here, which is good. It makes time go by faster, I think. Right now, we're primarily responsible for two towns. They each have their own personalities, which I'm trying to figure out, but I already have some goals I'd like to accomplish while I have responsibility and influence in them. The smaller town has a problem with sewage. Basically they have a drainage ditch of sewage that runs right through the middle of their town. I'm working with a Civil Affairs group and the local leadership to get something started that will provide the town with work and a cleaner town. Regardless, I hope to make positive changes and empower the local leaders in the towns to take responsibility for issues that seem basic to us. We feel safe in the towns and the local leaders assure us that we should, so that's a good thing, but we still stay on guard and keep focused at all times.

5. MIKE VALENTINE

Two weeks into his first deployment, Lieutenant Mike Valentine felt good about most aspects of his unit's RIP/TOA into sector, but one thing was bothering him. He decided to act on it.

At the conclusion of a company leadership meeting, Valentine approached his commander. His platoon sergeant and a fellow platoon leader stood with him as support.

"What's up, guys?" asked his CO.

"Sir," said Mike, "Can you hear us out on Battle Position 451? We all think it deserves re-visiting."

The commander slowly shook his head but kept listening.

"Sir," Valentine said, "After the TOA, the BP will be manned with our Bradleys, which don't have the commander's independent viewers that the outgoing unit's Bradleys have. In their Bradleys, the crew has 360-degree visibility, day and night, independent of the main gun sight. We won't have that with our Brads. There will be dead space behind and between our vehicles that will leave them vulnerable. We're just asking for your permission to adjust the vehicle positions on the BP to eliminate the blind spots."

"You know we can't do that," his commander replied. "The guidance from Higher is clear. We adopt all the TTPs of the outgoing unit for at least the first 30 days. Then we can assess them and decide if we want to change anything. There's a good reason for that policy."

"With all due respect, sir," interjected the platoon sergeant, "I've been on Bradleys for 15 years and I don't see how we can secure that position the way they have it without the commander's independent viewers."

"Sergeant, I fought from Kuwait to Baghdad to Fallujah in a Bradley," countered the commander. "I know how they work. But I also know that we're in the Army. Work with the current TTP for 30 days, and then I'll be more than willing to hear what you recommend, based on what you've learned on the ground here and now. Every rotation is different."

Two days later—on the first day that his unit's vehicles were manning the BP—Valentine was returning from a mounted patrol when he heard the first reports.

"Massive explosion reported vicinity BP 451 . . . no communications with the crew . . . Bradley engulfed in flames."

Three Soldiers—two from Valentine's company, one from the outgoing unit—were killed in the attack. Insurgents had slipped an anti-tank mine underneath the Bradley.

6. MIKE FABER

Typical mess hall sights, sounds, and smells greeted Lieutenant Mike Faber's senses as he walked between the tables.

It was all familiar to him. Mess halls seemed to be the same everywhere—including the mess hall conversations. A Soldier is complaining about a policy. A few others are poking fun back and forth. Faber recognized a few of his own Soldiers and took the opportunity to walk past their table—a chance to get a sense of his new platoon's morale.

A particularly rowdy bunch of Soldiers caught his attention. In the center of the group, a private held a slice of ham in the air, dangling it in the face of his buddies.

Faber gathered from the few words he heard that the Soldiers were discussing throwing ham at the Iraqi kids while on patrol. The ham-wielding private mimicked looks of horror and shock. The table erupted into laughter.

Faber stopped walking. He turned to face the group. The young Soldiers' banter subsided.

Faber took a seat at the table. After a few moments, the new platoon leader broke the awkward silence.

"Someone want to tell me what's so funny?"

7. STEPHANIE GILLESPIE

Lieutenant Stephanie Gillespie was being sent to take charge of a platoon that had not been led by an officer for five years.

"Ma'am," explained her command sergeant major, "The Soldiers need leadership. They have earned the unfortunate reputation of being undisciplined, to include poor uniform discipline outside the wire. They can be better than what they have shown so far."

"Roger, Sergeant Major," she replied. "I appreciate your insights."

The morning of her platoon's first mission after her arrival, Gillespie took the patrol leader aside and reminded him of the uniform standard—Kevlar, IBA, DAPs for gunners, gloves, eye and hearing protection, elbow and knee pads.

Several hours later, the Soldiers showed up for their patrol brief and rehearsal. The only protective gear they carried was their Kevlars and IBA.

Gillespie could feel her heartbeat increase. She called the patrol leader aside and reminded him that the Soldiers had to wear complete uniforms on the mission.

"It can't happen, ma'am," said the NCO. "There's not time; we can't miss SP."

The mission was set to begin in two hours, and the platoon's barracks were a mile away from the motor pool they were assembled in.

"It can't *not* happen," insisted Gillespie as calmly as she could. "You know the uniform standard. I reminded you of the standard earlier today. And it's your job to enforce the standard, Sergeant. You have trucks to move everyone back and forth to the company area. There is time to get in uniform and accomplish the mission. Now stop arguing with me and do your job."

The scene back at the barracks was chaotic. Stephanie saw Soldiers scrambling to the platoon connex to unpack gear from their locked duffel bags. She heard their frustrated voices: "I need knee pads, man, anyone got a knee pad? . . . Who took my fucking gloves? . . . Can I get a hand putting on these DAPS?"

It was painfully clear that these Soldiers had not worn the prescribed uniform in a long time, if ever.

At the SP, the patrol moved out, on time, in uniform, for once.

8. BRIAN LEBIEDNIK

Lieutenant Brian Lebiednik knocked on the door again. It was his first-ever house search in Iraq, and the resident had just slammed the door in his face.

Lebiednik knocked again. The man returned to the door, obviously perturbed. Lebiednik's interpreter restated their purpose there. The house owner seemed reluctant in stepping aside, but he allowed the American lieutenant to enter.

Lebiednik strode into the home and then stopped as if he'd forgotten something. He looked at the doorway just behind him. He saw, and smelled, his footprints leading from the door to where he stood. Sewage residue.

"I'm sorry about that," he said to his interpreter, who passed the message to the house owner. The man responded with gestures indicating that it didn't matter. Nonetheless, Lebiednik realized that tracking human trash and excrement into someone's house isn't good for winning hearts and minds.

"Are there any weapons in your house?" Lebiednik asked. The local shook his head, *no*.

"Well, we have to do a quick search anyway. Please move your family and all other personnel outside the house." His translator converted the message and the Iraqi moved upstairs, corralled his family, and led a line of women and children outside. Lebiednik signaled his platoon to start searching.

Within seconds of searching, one of his Soldiers came downstairs with an infant in his arms.

"Sir, I think the man might want his baby," the Soldier joked to his PL.

Lebiednik summoned the homeowner again.

"Why didn't you take your child outside when I told you to move your family outside? The child could have been hurt."

After translation, the Iraqi returned a confused expression.

"For the record, this counts as a person, too," Lebiednik said, handing the child over to the local. The man took his child outside, and the search resumed.

Minutes later, several Soldiers came down the stairs, carrying a stack of various weapons. Lebiednik called his interpreter and summoned the eldest male yet again.

"Why didn't you tell me there was a Kalashnikov in here? You said you had no weapons."

The Iraqi stumbled through his reply. The interpreter pieced it together and summarized the stammering: "He says it's for personal protection. It's not a weapon."

"Can you tell me what this is?" Lebiednik asked, pointing at the shotgun. His translator answered without consulting the local.

"That's for hunting," he said. "When you say 'weapon,' he thinks you mean 'pistol' for executing people."

Lebiednik rubbed his temples, and thought through every possible phraseology that might avoid the confusion.

"Ask him if he has anything else in the house that can be used to kill people."

Once again: *no*.

Lebiednik sifted through the pile to a pellet gun. He looked up at the interpreter and the man without saying a word.

"That's for shooting birds that eat the fruit off their trees," the interpreter reported.

Lebiednik looked at the NCO who led the search.

"You didn't find any bombs up there, did you?" Lebiednik asked.

"Ha," he chuckled. "None, sir."

"Alright, let's get the hell outta here. Sheesh."

9. BEN WEAKLEY

Lieutenant Ben Weakley surveyed the scene before him on a steamy Baghdad night. A PLS truck stacked with Jersey Barriers marked the spot where the next section of wall would appear. An M-88 wrecker was positioned perpendicular to the tail end of the truck, acting as a crane to download each two-ton block of concrete. Weakley's Engineers were supervising an ad-hoc collection of transporters and mechanics who together were tackling a mission that none of them had trained for—surrounding residential neighborhoods with high concrete walls.

As Weakley talked with his platoon sergeant, a man's scream pierced the night.

"Aaaaahhhhhh!"

Barriers on the back of the PLS had tumbled, partially crushing a Soldier under two of them. He was one of the mechanics.

Without a word, Weakley's experienced platoon sergeant took charge of the rescue mission. The accident had knocked the steel cable off the M-88's guide-wire spool, so the cable could not be used to lift the barrier.

"Get breaker bars and tanker bars," the platoon sergeant ordered. Soldiers scrambled to their vehicles and returned with the bars. Teams tried to re-align the guide wire on the M-88's crane and to create some breathing space for the trapped Soldier, but both efforts were unsuccessful. The Soldier was slowly suffocating.

Weakley reported the situation to his TOC and called a 9-line for medical evacuation.

"First Squad," ordered the platoon sergeant, "Bring up your ESV and use the blade to push the barrier off him." The Engineer Stryker Vehicle had a bulldozer-like blade on its front. First Squad rushed into action. The squad leader operated the vehicle. A team leader jumped up on the PLS to comfort his wounded comrade and to position the ESV's blade.

The squad leader inched the blade into position against the barrier. Soldiers grabbed hold of the casualty. As soon as the blade moved the barrier, the Soldiers pulled him free.

Weakley judged that the casualty was litter urgent. There was no time to wait for the helicopter MEDEVAC.

"We'll CASEVAC him directly to the CSH," he ordered. "Put him in the back of the ESV and let's go!"

The Stryker didn't move.

"First Squad, let's go!" he repeated. Then he saw what was causing a delay. The movement of barriers that had freed the trapped mechanic had inadvertently trapped the team leader who had been assisting.

"I'm sorry. I'm so sorry," the squad leader who had operated the ESV was saying to his buddy, holding his free hand. "We'll get you out of here."

"Sergeant," Weakley told the squad leader, "We have to go to the CSH right now."

"I can't leave him. I won't leave him. Fuck all this!" cried the distraught squad leader.

"The mechanic is litter urgent, Sergeant. Let's go!" ordered Weakley.

The mechanic's CASEVAC convoy was waiting. The team leader's injury did not immediately threaten his life or limb.

"Oh, God, what have I done . . . ."

"Now!" the platoon leader commanded, looking directly into the tearing eyes of his battle-proven NCO. The message got through. The squad leader snapped up, ran to his waiting vehicle, and led the convoy to its destination.

The CASEVAC convoy sped to the CSH in minutes, saving the Soldier's life. The platoon sergeant was able to free the team leader, who suffered a broken hand.

Later that night, Weakley sat talking with his platoon sergeant in their CP back at the FOB. Neither of them could sleep.

The squad leader who had operated the ESV appeared in the doorway.

"Come on in," said Weakley.

The NCO remained standing in the doorway. Then, looking at his platoon leader, he said, "Sir, we all thought that if something bad happened you were going to freak out and get somebody killed. You proved us wrong tonight, LT."

It had taken a while, but Ben finally sensed that he had earned the trust of his platoon.

10. CLINT SPEEGLE

Lieutenant Clint Speegle and his company commander decided to fly their pair of Apaches over to Dora Farms as they waited to cover a convoy transporting a high-value target. Dusk had already fallen.

They eased around the dull outline of the nuclear power plant in southeast Baghdad and then started flying back across the silver ribbon of river below. Speegle was flying in the front seat of the trail aircraft, scanning under his night vision goggles; his back-seater was flying FLIR.

Speegle saw some flashes out his left window.

"Dude, I got some flashes, man," he said.

A moment later, the sky around the helicopter lit up with tracers.

"We got tracers. We got big fucking tracers coming at us!"

Speegle realized they had flown into the middle of a triangle-shaped ambush; the enemy was firing from three directions.

"Break left! Break right!"

Speegle pressed his hands and face against the window, looking for the ground threat.

The enemy gunners followed their every move.

"Break left."

The gunfire followed the aircraft.

"Bump up and right."

The gunners followed them.

Speegle scanned around his aircraft, searching for his wingman. He couldn't locate him.

He saw a target on the ground, one of the enemy gunners. Speegle switched to the FLIR. Just as he pulled his machine gun's trigger, his commander's aircraft came into view—flying right into the arc of his rounds streaming toward the target. Speegle cringed and prayed that the rounds wouldn't hit his commander's aircraft. Somehow, they missed.

Speegle checked the ground for signs of a target. He couldn't find one. Then there was nothing. They were out of the ambush.

Speegle's company commander broke the tension.

"Ooh, *that's* a CAB," he said.

They both chuckled over the net, trying to regain their composure.

MONTH TWO

11. KEVIN STEIN

"Hadji in the silver Audi is checking us out," crackled over the platoon net.

Looking to his right, Lieutenant Kevin Stein saw the car paralleling his four-truck patrol. A lone Iraqi military-aged male occupied the late-model car, and he was indeed staring at the Humvee ahead of Stein's in the order of movement.

Suddenly, the Audi sped ahead of the patrol.

"Stop him, and let's see what he's so interested in," Stein ordered.

The American patrol accelerated, forcing the congested road traffic to move out of its way. Pulling up behind the Audi, the lead Humvee honked its horn, flashed its lights, and signaled for the driver to stop. But he didn't. The Audi swerved through traffic to escape the patrol, but the traffic parted like the Red Sea for the noisy, threatening gun trucks. The medium-speed chase eventually moved into a city center, with throngs of shoppers enjoying the cool evening air.

One of Stein's squad leaders had had enough of this.

"Lead gunner, fire to disable that fucking car," he ordered over the net.

Holy shit!

Stein keyed his platoon net as fast as he could.

"Do not shoot! Do not shoot," he ordered. "Way too many civilians in the area."

But the squad leader was right. They couldn't allow anyone to defy the authority of American forces like this.

"Blue Two," Stein ordered over the net to the lead truck. "Knock his bumper until he stops."

The tactic worked; the Audi finally stopped. Working through the platoon's interpreter, a squad leader questioned the sweating, youthful driver as Stein observed.

The tactical questioning revealed that the driver was a 17-year-old boy who had never before seen Americans up close. He had been told that Americans kidnapped and killed Iraqis. When Stein's Soldiers had all looked over at him, the boy assumed that they were going to kidnap him, so he fled for his life.

"Tell him we don't detain or harm Iraqis who obey the laws," Stein told his interpreter. "Although this idiot did almost get himself killed," he commented to his platoon sergeant as they returned to their trucks.

The platoon mounted up and resumed their patrol, unsure of what the teenager now thought of American Soldiers.

12. KARL SIMPKINS

Lieutenant Karl Simpkins made it a point to look into his Soldiers' eyes when they were outside the wire. His platoon patrolled mounted most of the time, but there were always opportunities for him to get on the ground and check up on his other trucks.

Looking into their eyes, he would see their pride, fear, confidence, exhaustion or any of the countless other emotions that war fuels. It helped Simpkins keep a pulse on his men as they adjusted to this deployment.

Whenever he looked into the eyes of one of his squad leaders, however, the only emotion he read was hatred. SSG Jimmelt, a veteran of an earlier rotation in Iraq, was someone that the platoon leader had been counting on to lead and teach the younger Soldiers. But his platoon wasn't going to win any hearts and minds by looking at Iraqis the way SSG Jimmelt did.

LT Simpkins approached his senior squad leader back on the FOB.

"Sergeant Jimmelt, how's morale?" said the PL with a smile.

"Not bad, sir," he replied. "It is what it is in Iraq."

"You know, Sergeant J," said Simpkins, "I'm counting on you to set the example for all the new guys, but I gotta tell you, out on patrol you look and act like you hate all the people here."

The NCO looked straight into his platoon leader's eyes.

"I do hate every mother-fucking raghead in this country," he said coolly. "I wish we'd leave and bomb this place into glass. But since we ain't gonna do that, I just need to make sure that me and my guys come home alive. All the people in this backward, disgusting country aren't worth one drop of American blood."

The grizzled NCO collected his thoughts.

"You'll see, sir," he continued with a hint of condescension. "I once believed all the hype like you do. You'll see."

That evening, Simpkins approached his battery commander. "Sir," he said. "I think we may have to do something with SSG Jimmelt. He really, really hates Iraqis. I'm afraid that he's a powder keg who could do something real bad if anything goes down."

"You think?" the captain replied sarcastically. "He was a major problem last deployment. We hoped he'd work through it. But it sounds like that didn't happen. I'm glad you brought this to my attention, Karl. Good call. I'll get with the First Sergeant and Sergeant Major and get him swapped out with an E-5 or E-6 from the guard force."

The next day, a new NCO reported to Simpkins' platoon.

13. DAVE MACPHAIL

The route-clearance platoon crept along at five miles per hour in its "domination formation." Operating late at night after curfew, the hulking vehicles—RG-31 MRAPs, Buffalos, Huskies, and up-armored Humvees—moved in parallel columns along both sides of the highway. Lieutenant Dave MacPhail's Humvee moved behind an RG-31 and in front of a Buffalo.

Whomp-WHHHHHOOOOOOOMMMM!

There was a bright flash of light, and then MacPhail saw the RG-31 lurch sideways and roll to a stop amid a cloud of smoke.

This was the first time his platoon had been hit by an IED, but the Soldiers had rehearsed endlessly for this moment.

MacPhail's Humvee moved forward of the stricken vehicle as the platoon established 360-degree security. After a quick check for secondary IEDs, the platoon's aid-and-litter team dismounted and moved to treat the wounded.

MacPhail stayed on the radio to send the SITREP and request a QRF and MEDEVAC.

"Apache base, this is Apache One-Six, over."

No response.

"Ironclaw base, this is Apache One-Six, over," he called.

His calls went unanswered. His platoon was too far away from both his company and battalion TOCs.

"We have three KIA and one litter urgent," came the initial report from his assistant patrol leader, a squad leader who was leading the casualty ops.

MacPhail switched frequencies and finally established communications with an American unit. That unit's TOC began to relay all of MacPhail's reports to his higher HQ.

Looking in his side-view mirror at the activities going on behind his truck, MacPhail watched as his medic treated the wounded Soldier. One of the dead Soldiers—whose legs had been shorn off—lay on the road behind the MRAP.

Then MacPhail observed the "dead" Soldier begin to move, twisting his trunk from side to side and raising his arms.

MacPhail jumped out of his truck.

"He's alive!" he yelled, pointing at the casualty. "Help him!"

Horrified, Soldiers from the aid-and-litter team rushed to their comrade and placed tourniquets on him, but he soon died.

The assistant patrol leader ran to MacPhail's truck.

"We got to CASEVAC SGT P right now—no time to wait for a MEDEVAC," he said breathlessly. "I'll put him in my truck and take the Buffalo for security."

After the CASEVAC convoy departed, MacPhail sat in his vehicle waiting for a QRF and a recovery team to arrive. The smoldering fire in the RG-31 began to grow larger. The realization of what had occurred began to sink in. He couldn't bear the thought of his Soldiers being burned in the flames—even if they were dead.

He tugged on his gunner's leg.

"Let's go get them out of there!" he said to the strongest Soldier in his truck.

The Humvee's driver moved up into the turret to pull security.

MacPhail led his gunner to the burning vehicle. The door on the back end of the MRAP was open with dark smoke pouring out. MacPhail pulled himself up to the doorway and entered the troop compartment. His boots slipped on the slick, blood-soaked surface. He immediately saw a Soldier wedged against the vehicle's hull, but the casualty was unrecognizable. Dave and his gunner grabbed onto the Soldier's IBA and began to pull, but the body was stuck.

"I'll grab his legs and push," MacPhail told his gunner.

When Dave moved to take hold of the Soldier's legs, he discovered that they weren't there. The mush of flesh he encountered offered no leverage. There was nothing they could do to dislodge the body.

Flames began licking at the rescuers.

"We got to get out of here, sir," his gunner said. "Rounds are going to start cooking off."

Dave was determined to protect at least one of his Soldier's remains. He moved forward in the compartment and grabbed hold of the driver, first under his arms to no avail, and then by his IBA loop. He pulled with all his strength, but again the Soldier didn't budge.

"Sir! Rounds are cooking off!" he heard his gunner yell through the smoke and flames.

Dave let go of his fallen Soldier and crawled down the length of the burning vehicle, tumbling out its back door onto the bloody highway.

For the next two hours, Dave and his Soldiers watched the RG-31 burn and listened to the ammunition inside it explode, knowing that two of their brothers were inside.

14. CHRIS DEFIORI

Lieutenant Chris DeFiori watched as his Soldiers assembled in the platoon area. He and his platoon sergeant had decided that it was time for a "sensing session" to help everyone—especially the new guys—deal with what had happened the night before.

Last night, several blasts and the staccato of automatic-weapons fire had rocked the neighborhood outside the FOB. DeFiori and his Soldiers were not the QRF, yet still they had rushed to the ECP to assist in any way they could. When the stricken convoy arrived at the FOB, DeFiori's Soldiers pulled the dead and wounded from the trucks, rushing them to the nearby aid station. For DeFiori's new Soldiers, it was the first time they had come face to face with the carnage of dead and severely wounded Americans. DeFiori had noticed the shocked expressions on some of his Soldiers' faces.

The platoon leader opened the sensing session.

"This is a chance for everyone to talk about what happened last night and about how you're feeling about the deployment so far," DeFiori said. "We've had some close calls, and last night was some fucked-up shit, and I know a lot of us are thinking that it could have easily been us. Anyway, nothing's out of bounds, and it's good to say whatever you're thinking and feeling."

The platoon sergeant spoke first. A veteran of three previous deployments to Iraq and Afghanistan, he was the most senior, most seasoned, most respected Soldier in the platoon.

"Hey, I'm scared as hell every time I go out there," he stated. "It's almost like you can't do anything about it, with the IEDs and EFPs. If they're going to get you, they're going to get you. I just do my best to find them and hope to stay lucky. I don't know how anyone wouldn't be afraid. But, you know, we do what Soldiers do. We deal with the fear and drive on to get the mission done."

DeFiori could sense the change as his platoon sergeant's words cut the tension in the room. The most experienced combat leader in the unit had expressed what everyone was feeling inside. He had normalized their inner feelings.

The sensing session lasted well over an hour, as almost everyone said something. By the time it was over, Chris DeFiori knew that his platoon was mentally ready to go back outside the wire.

15. JOE TOMASELLO

"Sir!" whispered the private, waking his platoon leader. "There's some activity down the road."

Lieutenant Joe Tomasello rose from the floor of the abandoned Iraqi house that his platoon was occupying. In the darkness, he moved swiftly out the door and through high grass up to the rural road where one of his gun trucks was guarding against night-time IED emplacers.

"It just appeared there," the squad leader explained to him. Through the night-vision device affixed to the M240B machine gun in the turret, Tomasello could see a light but no other activity approximately 300 meters down the road. That stretch of road was an IED hot spot.

"X-Ray, this is Delta Four-Six," radioed Tomasello to his battalion TOC. We see a light on the road about 300 meters east of our position. Do we have any friendlies there?"

He waited a minute or two for the reply.

"Negative, Delta Four-Six. No friendlies."

The rules of engagement permitted Tomasello's unit to engage anyone on that road at night.

"Shoot a burst," Tomasello ordered.

BUH-DUH-DUH-DUH-DUH!

The tracer indicated accurate fire, yet the light on the road didn't move at all.

"Hold your fire for now," Tomasello instructed the gunner. "But if you see anything moving out on the road, light him up."

A few moments later, the watchful silence was shattered as the battalion net came alive.

"Delta Four-Six, CEASE FIRE, CEASE FIRE!" called the TOC. "Alpha Company has a crater-overwatch position there! The light you see is the chem light they just placed on their concertina wire. DO NOT ENGAGE."

Tomasello looked over at the M240 gunner, who looked like he was about to throw up.

"Hey, man, you didn't do anything wrong. You did the right thing," his PL assured him. "The TOC and me fucked up, but not you."

16. CHRIS LARSEN

"The pick-up truck is back, over," came the report from the Bradley commander.

Lieutenant Chris Larsen could also see the area in question from his Humvee, although he was 800 meters away from the Bradley's battle position. He trusted the Bradley crew's judgment—they were closer to the suspects and it was still early enough in the morning for the Bradley thermal sights to clearly show the heat signatures. The report: two males, apparently back to prep a well-known IED hole for re-use.

Larsen had already alerted the QRF a few minutes prior when the truck had made a brief stop and then drove away.

"Now they're digging in the road and putting something on the ground, over," the Bradley commander said.

The ROE was clear: anyone digging in the road or emplacing something in the road was perceived a threat.

"If they're emplacing something in the road, then engage them," Larsen said.

He heard the Bradley rip off a short burst of fire at the suspected IED emplacers.

"Let's go check it out," he said.

Chris pulled his two Humvees out of their hide site and joined the Bradley en route to the engagement area.

When the vehicles rolled to a stop, Chris dismounted to investigate. He looked at the remains—smaller bodies than he had expected—just teenage boys. But the shovels, the gas cans, the copper wires strewn about confirmed the boys' intent.

Back at the FOB, Chris called the platoon together for an AAR. The Soldiers went over the incident, how they made the right decision, even though it led to unfortunate consequences for two men younger than everyone in the platoon. They tried to put the images of the shot-up teens behind them.

The next morning, Chris led a dismounted patrol through the streets of the village. He saw a crowd of about 25 people milling around behind a house. Chris recognized one of the men there, so he decided to greet the group.

"This man says they are gathering for a funeral," the interpreter told Chris. "He says you Americans have killed his sons."

The man kept pleading a repeated phrase to Chris's interpreter.

"He says the boys were just selling gas," the interpreter said.

Chris tried to explain to the man what happened—that they had been digging, that they had carried a shovel and wire—but the locals were speaking over his interpreter. The man remained adamant about his boys' innocence, and Chris returned to his platoon to continue the patrol.

Two weeks later, a team from Chris's platoon was hiding in a three-story building, waiting on the sun to rise and hoping to spot an enemy sniper team—a team that had inflicted three casualties on the company in the past few weeks.

The Soldiers had a good view of the town. Chris was surveying the scene from a separate room when his guys alerted him.

"Hey, sir, we got activity 200 meters to the west," a Soldier reported. "You should come check this out."

Chris and his team passed around the 60-power spotting scope to get a closer look. They saw what they'd been looking for: three guys unloading weapons from a black sedan. They saw an AK, a PKC, and an SKS.

"Are we clear, sir?"

"Engage," Larsen said.

Shots rang out from his team's M4s and an M24 sniper rifle. Two of the enemy fell dead under the attack. The driver somehow slipped away behind the car.

"There he goes! Hit him!"

"He's running toward that group of people. He's gonna go into that house!"

As Larsen moved to get a better view, he heard the firing stop.

"Hey, why'd you stop firing?" Larsen asked.

"Sir, there's a fucking kid right there!"

Chris looked through his scope to see an older woman dart out of the house and pull the child inside. The fleeing enemy had disappeared.

17. MEGAN WILLIAMS

Lieutenant Megan Williams sat across the desk from the Iraqi Police District Commander, a colonel. She was listening to one of his many stories about the Iran-Iraq War. The beaming smile on the burly colonel's mustachioed face expressed his appreciation for her interest in Iraq's history and for her rudimentary command of the Arabic language.

An Arab Studies major in college, Megan was now the Police Training Team advisor to this police district. She valued the relationships that developed out of talking about topics other than "police work."

"You look like an Arab woman," the police chief said to Megan as an obvious compliment.

"In fact, my family is Arabic," she replied.

The colonel looked ecstatic.

"From what country?" he asked.

Megan knew that he was a Shia. Based on her knowledge of the region, she selected a Shiite Arab country.

"Lebanon," she replied.

He was very pleased. "Lebanon is a nation of great history and people," he said, smiling at his new American friend.

Megan smiled back at him. It wasn't too big of a lie. Israel, after all, is close to Lebanon. And she never said that she wasn't Jewish; she merely allowed him to assume otherwise. For the success of the mission, some things were best left unsaid.

MONTH THREE

18. CRAIG ARNOLD

Lieutenant Craig Arnold's platoon was convoying along a rural stretch of Iraqi highway that was paralleled by earthen berms on both sides. The convoy's lead vehicle abruptly halted and began to back up.

"There's a command wire running over the berm on the left, leading to something suspicious along the roadway," reported the lead squad leader. Following their SOP, the platoon moved back away from the kill zone and scanned for any secondary IEDs.

Arnold saw one of his squads dismount and begin bounding towards the berm. That squad loved taking the fight to the enemy. From the top of the berm, the squad leader reported over his Icom radio to Arnold that the wire led to a shack. The squad disappeared over the berm.

"Hold your position and observe the shack. We'll bring up engineer assets," ordered Arnold. He briefed the platoon every day about baited ambushes.

There was no acknowledgement.

"Two-Two, this is Two-Six," he repeated. "Hold your position. Acknowledge, over."

Nothing.

"Gunners," Arnold called over the platoon net. "Wave flags to get second squad's attention. They need to hold where they are."

The gunners stood tall in their turrets and attempted to visually signal a halt, but the assaulting squad apparently was not looking back.

KA-BOOM!

Arnold felt the concussion before he saw the brown mushroom cloud.

Arnold ordered his platoon sergeant to lead the platoon to the blast site because his truck was equipped with electronic countermeasures against IEDs.

By the time the platoon linked up with the squad, one Soldier was already dead; another was severely wounded; the squad leader was unscathed physically but in shock mentally.

Arnold tried to call for a MEDEVAC. There was no response on the battalion and company nets. His platoon was situated in a communications dead zone, mid-way between their FOB to the north and their company headquarters to the south. Arnold managed to make contact with another coalition patrol that relayed his 9-line.

The MEDEVAC bird arrived quickly and whisked the wounded Soldier away.

And then there was silence.

Arnold's Soldiers found themselves standing in the middle of nowhere, with one of their brothers lying literally in pieces on the ground and another severely wounded and gone. They did not see any Iraqis; there was no sign of any insurgent. The Soldiers somberly policed up the remains of their brother, placing him in a body bag and moving him into the back seat of Arnold's Humvee for transport back to Mortuary Affairs at the FOB.

As they prepared to move out, Arnold received the relayed message from Higher: "Stay in place and secure the site until EOD arrives."

The platoon set up a perimeter around the area with two Humvees observing traffic on the highway. The Soldiers baked in the hot sun as they waited for EOD to get there.

"Sir," Arnold's driver said with a glance at the body bag, his voice cracking. "It ain't right for him to be out in the heat like this."

"It's not respectful," added his gunner.

"I don't like it either, guys," Arnold replied. "But we need to do our mission. Sergeant W's in a better place than us now anyway."

"Two-Six," came a radio call from one gun truck overwatching the highway. "There's a white car coming from the north, acting strange, slowing down. Request permission to engage."

"Negative," Arnold replied quickly.

He sensed a need to provide guidance to his angry, frustrated Soldiers.

"A driver slowing down when he sees an American gun truck along the highway," he reminded his platoon over the radio, "is acting normally. We're all pissed off, but we need to stay professional. We'll get SGT W back to the FOB as soon as we can."

19. CURTIS MINOR

Lieutenant Curtis Minor was relaxing in his company area late in the afternoon on a "refit day" when a battalion A/S-3 rushed in.

"Lieutenant Minor, the J-lens just watched some bad guys fire mortars at us," he said. "It looked like they left on foot without the mortar base plate. You need to get out there ASAP and check out the POO. It would be great to police up that base plate."

Less than 30 minutes later, Curtis was on the move outside the wire. His ad-hoc patrol consisted of nine American Soldiers—including him, his platoon sergeant, a forward observer, the battalion S-2, and a medic—and four Iraqi Army soldiers. The patrol moved by foot because there were no roads leading to the location. The insurgents had attacked from a farm field that was cris-crossed with irrigation canals and thus inaccessible to vehicles.

As soon as they arrived at the POO, the Soldiers found a cache of mortar rounds dug into the wall of a canal. A little further down the canal, they came across a cache of computer hard drives, cameras, and video tapes. The S-2 was thrilled. Soon after, a Soldier identified a huge cache of home-made explosives. "We found their mother lode, baby!" he exclaimed.

Curtis wondered if it were too much of a good thing. His small patrol had stumbled across a major enemy asset, one that was too large to leave unsecured yet also too large to hand-carry back to the patrol base.

Looking around, Curtis identified a simple farmhouse at the near side of a small hamlet. The women and children there looked nervous. Curtis felt an uneasiness in his gut.

"We're going to occupy that house and establish a hasty defense until we can get more resources out here to exploit the caches," he ordered.

As they occupied the house, Curtis heard a report from the rooftop: "There are guys moving in and out of reeds about 200 meters northwest."

Curtis moved to the roof with his FO, who started plotting coordinates and radioing them back to the battalion mortar platoon.

SNAP!

Curtis could feel the sniper round as it zinged past his face. The next thing he knew he was laying flat on the roof. Gunfire erupted all around him. He grabbed his FO and pulled him into the stairwell.

"I'm hit!" cried the machinegun's assistant gunner, falling back on the rooftop. The machine gunner dragged his buddy off the rooftop and down the stairs, leaving a trail of blood.

"The gun's damaged and no good," he told his PL as he pushed past.

Curtis called a SITREP and the 9-line for a MEDEVAC.

"Air is Red," replied the battalion TOC. "Birds can't fly due to sandstorms. You'll have to CASEVAC."

Curtis moved downstairs to the living room, where the medic was treating the wounded Soldier. A round had traveled through the Soldier's bicep and lodged in his chest, striking him in his side above the SAPI plate. The medic judged the wound serious but stabilized.

Curtis broke the glass in the living room window and began returning fire. His platoon sergeant did the same in a bedroom. With the loss of the machinegun, maintaining fire parity required everyone to become a rifleman.

WUMP! WUMP!

Friendly mortar rounds began falling on enemy positions. First the company's 60mm mortars arrived, and then the battalion's 120mm mortars, and both fires were accurate. The enemy's attack ceased almost immediately.

Curtis didn't want to give the enemy time to re-organize.

"Exfil to the patrol base," he ordered. "Prep the casualty for movement. Where's the SKEDCO litter?"

His Soldiers' blank stares answered his question. In the rush to start the mission, PCIs had not been conducted.

Curtis looked around for something to use as a field-expedient litter. He saw the S-2, who was holding a blanket he had taken from a bedroom to safeguard the cache's hard drives.

"We're going to need that blanket," Curtis told him. The S-2 opened the blanket and laid it on the floor. It would carry their wounded comrade *and* the enemy's hard drives.

Curtis threw smoke grenades to conceal the patrol's exfiltration. Two Soldiers moved out first as lead security. Four Soldiers carried the casualty. Two Soldiers moved behind as rear security. The Iraqi soldiers tagged along, unwilling to assist.

Movement was painfully slow. Darkness had fallen. Boots sunk deep into the plowed farm fields. The blanket did not have handles, and the litter-bearers' forearms and hands soon ached.

Curtis swapped Soldiers between carrying the casualty and pulling security. He sent SITREPs to Higher and coordinated for an ambulance exchange point at the closest possible location—1,500 meters away from the farmhouse. He exhorted his men to carry on: "You can do it. Keep it up. We'll get him to the hospital."

They came to a 10-foot wide, 4-foot deep irrigation canal. As they slid down its muddy slope, the litter bearers strained to pull the blanket up to their chests. The grip of one Soldier slipped.

"I can't do it," he cried. The litter began to sink in the dark water.

"Don't let me drown! Don't let me drown!" screamed the wounded Soldier as he looked up at a black sky and felt himself sinking into the water.

Curtis rushed forward and took hold of the blanket. He realized that although he had done "litter PT" on many occasions, he had never done it with a wet blanket, up muddy embankments and across plowed fields, while wearing full combat gear, and with a Soldier's life at stake.

Ninety minutes after departing from the objective, the CASEVAC patrol arrived at the vehicle link-up point. No one was there.

"Where are you?" he radioed his fellow platoon leader.

"I'm at the linkup point," he said. "Where are you?"

Curtis popped a star cluster.

"Got it. On the way," reported his friend.

Nothing had ever sounded better to Curtis than the sound of the approaching Humvees. His Soldiers placed their wounded brother across the backseat of a Humvee that sped off into the night. LT Curtis Minor and his Soldiers then walked the final 300 meters back to the patrol base.

20. DAN RIORDAN

Lieutenant Dan Riordan's two lead trucks cordoned off the north end of the road, and his rear trucks covered the south. The platoon had the suspicious vehicle surrounded. Riordan checked his comms.

"Seven, this is Six, radio check, over."

He waited a moment.

"White Seven, this is White Six, over."

Still no answer.

Riordan stepped out of his truck, cupped his hands around his mouth and screamed.

"Platoon Sergeant, turn on your radio!"

He waited for his platoon sergeant's voice.

"White Six, this is White Seven, over." It was the platoon sergeant.

"Roger, keep that radio on," Riordan said. "Do you see anything on the vehicle from there, over?"

Riordan glanced at it again. The vehicle appeared to sit low on its rear tires, a key indicator that it could be loaded with explosives.

"Nothing besides the load in the trunk," the platoon sergeant said.

Riordan thought through his options.

Then he heard the faint grumble of a Humvee accelerating in the distance. He looked up and saw his platoon sergeant pulling away from the cordon and rolling into the town.

"Where on earth are you going?" Riordan asked over the radio. The platoon sergeant's vehicle turned out of sight.

No response.

Another one of his truck commanders got on radio.

"Sir, I can see his truck. He's about three blocks into the village. I think he's chasing someone down."

Riordan tried to reach him on the radio a few more times, with no success.

After about five minutes, the PSG's truck rolled back to the convoy, driving right up to Riordan's truck. Riordan dismounted.

"Turn on your radio, Sergeant," he said. "What did you think you were doing?"

His platoon sergeant twisted in his seat and pointed to a detainee in the back of his Humvee.

Riordan knew the Soldiers were watching this conversation. He leaned in through the window of the truck.

"This isn't Hollywood, Sergeant," he said. "We'll talk about this back at the FOB."

21. JIM GUGGENHEIM

Lieutenant Jim Guggenheim surveyed the buildings around his position, searching for possible sniper locations. The shots had been close, but fortunately, no casualties.

The most likely point of origin for the shots was a house a block away. The S-2 had already templated it as a possible enemy sniper location.

Guggenheim reported the engagement and ordered his men to investigate the house with caution.

"Sir, we're seeing wires coming from the house, leading to a propane tank, over."

Possible booby trap.

"All right," Guggenheim said, "I'm calling up some air support to check the roof."

Guggenheim had hoped for Apaches. Battalion was pushing to set up a JDAM strike. Guggenheim was told to hold his position until the bombing was complete.

Just before the jets were ready to drop bombs, Guggenheim's men gave another report on the house:

"Sir, we just saw a woman come out of the house."

Guggenheim put a hold on the bombing. He decided to clear the house with his own men instead.

As the Soldiers approached the house, they saw that the wires weren't actually leading to the propane tanks like they had thought. The Soldiers proceeded to enter and clear the house.

There were two men inside the house—father and son—and they had weapons. The Soldiers detained them. After a few minutes of tactical questioning, the detainees admitted to shooting at the Americans, but claimed that they were protecting their home from what they thought were robbers.

Guggenheim asked for their names, to which they gave a prompt reply. The PL recognized both names from the Black List.

22. MIKE RASH

At about 0700 on a sunny morning, Lieutenant Mike Rash was just half an hour away from completing his first official patrol as a new platoon leader. The patrol was nothing new for his platoon, which had already been in country for three months.

The patrol of three Humvees crossed a main road into the next neighborhood.

The lead vehicle had just turned left to head north as Mike's truck approached the same intersection. He looked south to see if they were clear.

A hot flash blasted through the cab of Mike's truck.

Mike was launched from the vehicle and found himself sliding on his back across the road like a Frisbee skipping across the pavement. After he slid to a stop, he saw a familiar object flying directly at him. The object slammed into his ACH, coming to rest about 5 meters away. Mike saw that it was the M240 machine gun off the top of his truck.

Mike's hearing was a dull roar. He frisked himself for wounds. Distant sounds returned, those of faint machine gun fire. Mike raised to a knee and scanned the buildings on the side of the street.

That's when he realized he'd been blown 25 meters away from his Humvee. He saw his truck sitting still and crooked, at the base of a gray-brown mushroom cloud of dust and smoke. He ran to the truck to check the crew.

"Is everybody okay? Everybody okay?"

An NCO was screaming, "Driver down! Driver down!"

Mike ran around to the driver's side of the Humvee. His driver was splayed on the ground, both of his legs gone, ripped off in the blast. Mike called for the platoon medic.

The NCO looked at his new platoon leader.

"I got it, sir," he said. "I'll get him."

The NCO ran to get the medic out of another vehicle. The medic moved up and started applying tourniquets. He stopped the bleeding.

They received fire from the north, bullets impacting all around them. The two other vehicles in the patrol maneuvered to provide cover, firing at insurgents on rooftops. Bullets peppered around Mike's disabled Humvee and the rescue group.

Mike was returning fire to the northeast when he came under fire from the southwest. His platoon was caught in an L-shaped ambush.

Mike called Higher for the QRF and decided to CASEVAC his driver immediately to medical care.

The platoon's vehicle gunners returned fire to both sides. Soldiers got the wounded driver into the lead vehicle for evacuation. As his driver was carried away, Mike continued to direct his platoon in battle, wondering if his driver would survive.

23. RYAN HARBICK

Lieutenant Ryan Harbick sat on a couch in a typical Iraqi home, talking with an elderly Iraqi man about security in the neighborhood. His platoon's clearing mission would end within the hour, and Ryan was happy to allow the home's atypically effective air conditioning to dry some of the sweat he'd worked up over the past 13 hours.

His conversation was interrupted by a radio call. "Legion Two-Six, Legion Six." His company commander calling for him.

"Legion Six, this is Two-Six."

"I need you to clear the field directly to your west. We've been having reports from the locals that insurgents like to place caches in there, and Battalion really wants us to search it before we head back to the FOB and it's too dark."

"Roger," replied Harbick. "Will we be getting any additional assets to help us in the search?"

"Negative, the Engineers are currently about two clicks north with Bravo Company, already being utilized. Be sure to use your metal detectors to make sure they don't have anything buried out there."

"Six, Two-Six, Roger."

Harbick called a squad leader who was upstairs in the house to come down and join him. He also radioed his platoon sergeant, who was a few houses away in another house with another squad. Once those two NCOs arrived, Harbick briefed his plan.

"All right," he said. "The CO just tasked us with clearing this field to the west. Locals report that the field has caches of explosives in it at various points. So what we'll do is put 2nd Squad to the north of the field and 3rd to the west of the field, to provide overwatch and look for any triggermen. 1st Squad and I will go into the field to search for the caches. Let's make sure we get the metal detectors off the Stryker before we get out there."

"Sir," suggested the squad leader. "Any chance we could *drive* the Stryker out in the field? I mean, all day we've been finding random arty rounds lying around. If we're dismounted, all it would take is one triggerman and we'll find that cache in a way we don't want."

"No," replied Harbick. "The Stryker wouldn't make it far in that field before it got stuck, and then we're dismounted anyways. We'll have to do this on foot."

"Well, all right, sir," said the squad leader, "but it sounds like a plan for us to get sent home early . . . in body bags, but early all the same."

"Fuck, give me a second to think," said Harbick. His NCOs' grave faces indicated their concerns with the plan. About three hours earlier, the XO's vehicle had been hit by an IED. Nobody had been hurt, but everybody knew there were plenty more IEDs out there. Nobody wanted to find them dismounted, especially if an Engineer Buffalo could find them without exposing anybody.

"So, you two think this is a bad plan, huh?" Harbick asked.

His platoon sergeant weighed in on the discussion.

43

"Sir, I just think the CO got the order and didn't think it through before he tasked us," he said. "We'll do it, but fuck, seems like a very unnecessary risk to me."

Harbick knew he was right. Somewhere inside he'd known all along that the plan was bad, but he'd gotten too caught up in getting the mission done. He keyed his radio.

"Legion Six, this is Two-Six."

"Six."

"Sir, we're ready to execute, but it seems like a pretty big unnecessary risk. The area is too large to have overwatch on everything. If we're dismounted, it'll take just one triggerman and we'll be picking up a fire team with a mop and scrub brushes. We know they've got IEDs in place. Charlie Company is going to have overwatch of the field tonight. Any chance we can have the Engineers in their Buffaloes check the field out tomorrow morning?"

The radio net went silent. Harbick, his platoon sergeant, and the squad leader exchanged glances. They had accomplished a lot of tough missions together. They waited.

"Two-Six, this is Six," the CO responded. "Roger, you're right. Hold off on that mission. I'll call Battalion and we'll get the Engineers out with you tomorrow morning. Six out."

The three leaders moved out to complete their 14-hour clearing mission with a little extra pep in their steps.

24. JON SHERRILL

Lieutenant Jon Sherrill's platoon was traveling down Route Cardinals on the way to an IP station when they were flagged down by an Iraqi traffic policeman. He claimed there might be an IED at the next intersection.

Sherrill gave orders and the platoon went into action. The Soldiers cordoned the intersection and established traffic control points. They put out traffic cones and wire. Sherrill called EOD to come investigate.

For the next six hours, Sherrill's men handled the traffic flow, directing cars around the cones and telling pedestrians to stay away.

The EOD element finally arrived, cleared the IED, and then continued to another mission. Sherrill's platoon had executed everything according to the SOP without a problem—except for the one Humvee that now wouldn't start.

"Sir, we're gonna need a slave cable over here to get this truck going again."

"Roger."

Sherrill ordered his men to break down their TCPs and collapse the cordon while the Humvee was being restarted.

Sherrill and his driver retrieved the wire and cones in front of their own truck. As Sherrill's driver was getting back into his Humvee, a sniper's bullet tore into his torso, just above the side plate of his body armor.

Sherrill snapped to cover and scanned down his sights, sweeping the buildings all around, waiting for a second shot. It never came.

Sherrill moved to his wounded driver and lifted him into the truck. Grabbing the hand mike, Jon issued a FRAGO to his platoon. "My driver's been hit by a sniper," Sherrill told them. "We don't have time to slave that truck. Just hook up a tow strap."

Sherrill ordered another Soldier to get behind the wheel of the truck and climbed into the back seat beside his driver, who was lying across the seats and not breathing. As the vehicles drove away,

Jon performed CPR on his driver, a Soldier he'd known and worked alongside for over two years, since their days in Korea.

The trail of Humvees bolted through the streets, honking their horns and waving traffic away. An NCO called ahead to the ECP to ensure fast entrance through the gate.

Sherrill continued CPR. His convoy was knocking Iraqi cars out of the way in its rush to the CSH.

Another report came over the platoon net.

"We have to stop, over. The tow strap broke."

The Soldiers worked frantically to get the second tow strap hooked up. For Sherrill performing CPR in the back of his Humvee, the delay seemed to take forever.

"Okay, we're good! Rolling!" came over the net.

A few blocks down the road, the second tow strap also broke.

"We gotta stop again, over. Broken strap."

"Fuck!"

Sherrill kept trying to revive his driver while his platoon worked to hook up the broken truck. It was their last tow strap.

Sherrill continued CPR, not sure if it was doing anything to help this Soldier he'd come to love.

"We're up. Moving out, over."

When they finally reached the CSH, Sherrill and others off-loaded their wounded brother and moved him inside. After a few minutes of frantic effort by the medical personnel there, one of the docs stopped and lifted his eyes.

"He's dead."

25. MIKE STEELE

Lieutenant Mike Steele and his route-clearance platoon came across a dead, bloated donkey along the MSR. The carcass could be used to hide an IED, so they knew that they had to dispose of it. The only practical way to dispose of something this size was to blow it up with C4.

After checking the donkey to insure that it was not booby-trapped, Steele's platoon sergeant gave the order over the radio for Soldiers to come forward and blow it up in place.

"Let's not blow it here," Steele said. "We're right in front of this apartment building. Use the plow to push it ahead 200 meters to the open spot."

His platoon sergeant disagreed. "Six, look how bloated this thing is," he said over the platoon radio net. "It we push it, it will likely explode from all the gasses built up inside. Dead-donkey guts will get all over the plow and it'll smell like crap. Blow it in place here."

Steele keyed his radio again. "An explosion here will shatter all the windows in the building, and people live in those apartments," he explained. "We see children here every time we clear this route."

"Bombs go off all the time in this city," argued his platoon sergeant. "And this place is already dirty as hell. We should blow it here and get moving again."

"Negative, end of discussion," ordered Steele. "2nd Squad, drop your plow, push the donkey 200 meters down the road, and blow it there."

"Roger," acknowledged the 2nd Squad Leader.

MONTH FOUR

26. TREVOR BUCKEY

It was five o'clock in the morning, the raid was complete, and the detainee had been successfully transferred to the holding area. For Lieutenant Trevor Buckey's platoon, all that remained was a safe drive home to the base.

The Humvees began turning around to head out the gate into sector.

FUMP!!

"What the hell was that?"

One of the Humvee gunners in the convoy had inadvertently discharged a 40mm HE round into a Hesco barrier five meters away. The round did not detonate.

Every eye seemed to turn to the platoon leader in the expanse of silence. Then the guys started urging him to overlook the incident.

"Sir, no harm done."

Buckey sat in silence.

"He was just clearing it, sir. That's what this area's for."

"Sir, you know he'll get an Article 15."

Buckey knew it could take hours for EOD to come clear the new UXO, and the platoon needed to rest before the next day's missions. Buckey knew the book answer on this one. He made a decision.

"Let's head back to base," he said. "It's been a long enough night."

Midway back to his compound, Buckey was still thinking about the negligent discharge. He righted himself in his seat and keyed his hand mike.

"Eagle base, this is Alpha Two-Six. I have a serious incident to report, over."

27. BRIAN LARSON

Lieutenant Brian Larson knew his brigade's SOP for a traffic control point: if the TCP were expected to last longer than 20 minutes, the unit had to emplace signs, traffic cones, and concertina wire. Those measures reduced the likelihood of innocent Iraqis approaching a TCP at high speeds and being mistaken for SVBIEDs and killed. However, the SOP had the unintended consequence of increasing the threat from enemy sniper fire.

The insurgents had quickly figured out that when the Americans put out cones and wires, they not only would be stationary for at least 20 minutes, but they also would have to recover their equipment. The day before, a Soldier in another unit had been killed on this same stretch of road while recovering concertina wire at a TCP. The sniper had engaged him with a "keyhole" shot and escaped.

So when one of Larson's Bradleys broke down on the road, he consciously disobeyed the SOP. He figured that he was paid to exercise judgment. At this location, he reasoned, the risk of enemy sniper fire outweighed the risk of non-combatant casualties.

As his platoon sergeant worked to recover the immobile Bradley, Larson established a protective cordon with two Humvees, one covering each avenue of approach. Twice, his Soldiers had to fire warning shots with their M4 rifles to convince an oncoming vehicle to find a different route to its destination.

The cordon had lasted almost an hour when Larson saw a white sedan approaching the cordon at high speed. The gunner on a Humvee signaled with his arms for the car to halt; it did not. The driver flashed the vehicle's lights; the sedan kept speeding closer.

"Fire a warning shot," Larson ordered when the vehicle was 100 meters away and closing fast.

The gunner did so, but the car appeared to speed up.

"Engage!" Larson ordered.

Rounds from a turret-mounted M240 machinegun spewed into the speeding car. Another Soldier opened fire with a shotgun, exploding the sedan's tires. Other Soldiers fired with their M4s into the car, which finally rolled to a stop less than 5 meters from the Humvee that engaged it.

The Soldiers braced for an explosion. Nothing.

Larson called his platoon sergeant to come forward in his Bradley to investigate the car. Pulling alongside the car, his platoon sergeant peered into the vehicle.

"Oh, shit, this ain't good," he reported. "The guy inside is dead . . . and he's old . . . and I mean real old, with thick glasses."

With the Bradley protecting them, a dismounted squad began to clear the vehicle.

"Not only are his glasses as thick as Coke bottles," observed the squad leader, "but he's got hearing aids in both ears. He couldn't see or hear shit."

At the conclusion of the mission, back at the FOB, Larson led an AAR for his platoon while his battalion XO observed. After leading his Soldiers through a step-by-step reconstruction of what had occurred, Larson felt compelled to assure them.

"The situation here is terrible," he explained. "That old man was just in the wrong place at the wrong time. Hell, he shouldn't have even been out on the road, as blind and deaf as he was. Given the information we had, everyone did the right thing. If we face this situation again, do not hesitate to fire. If anything, we need to shoot earlier. If that had been an SVBIED, 1st Squad would all be dead right now."

The XO concurred that the incident was a tragedy of war, and that everyone had done the right thing. He backed up Larson's decision not to emplace TCP markers.

Two weeks later, however, after a 15-6 investigation and a public condemnation of the incident by the local Neighborhood Advisory Council, Larson was given a Letter of Admonishment by his battalion commander for not adhering to the brigade's SOP.

28. CHRIS FORD

Lieutenant Chris Ford and his platoon had the mission to record the Friday prayers at a particular mosque. The platoon leader selected a nearby house and knocked on its door. A man opened the door.

"Salaam alaykum," Ford greeted him. The man replied in kind.

Speaking in short clips through his interpreter, Ford explained the situation.

"I am Lieutenant Ford from the American Army . . . My Soldiers and I will need to be in your house for several hours . . . I apologize for any inconvenience . . . First we will need to look through your house . . . No family members will be permitted to leave while we are here . . . If you would like a few minutes to prepare your household, I will wait."

The Iraqi man nodded his understanding and closed the door.

The man soon re-appeared and welcomed the Soldiers in. The Soldiers kicked the dirt off their boots before entering. Ford's platoon conducted a soft, "level-one" search, being careful not to damage anything. Ford noticed that all the women had moved to a room behind a curtain.

After the house had been cleared and secured, a team of Ford's Soldiers moved to the roof. They crawled across the flat concrete, staying low to avoid being observed, and set up their audio-recording equipment. Downstairs inside the house, the homeowner pulled out chairs for Ford, his platoon sergeant, and himself, and together they drank *chai*, a sweetened tea.

"You have a beautiful home," Ford began, and the three of them enjoyed a conversation about their respective families.

A short while later, family members emerged from the kitchen carrying plates of freshly prepared chicken and rice for all of Ford's Soldiers. Ford watched as one of the man's sons delivered meals to the Soldiers on the roof. The boy low-crawled on his belly to each Soldier's hidden position, carefully pushing the plate of food ahead of him.

"I cannot thank you enough for your generosity," Ford said to the man, gesturing with his right hand over his heart.

When the Friday prayers were over and the mosque-monitoring mission complete, Ford reminded his platoon sergeant to insure that the platoon left everything in the house in the same condition it was when they entered it.

As the platoon began to depart, the man thanked the Soldiers for their thoughtfulness.

"We are friends now," he stated. "You are always welcome in my house."

29. BRYAN CROSSMAN

Lieutenant Bryan Crossman suspected that his position had been compromised the last time his platoon had monitored this particular mosque; especially since the Friday prayer had been less provocative than the intel had predicted. This time, Crossman intended to be more stealthy.

The platoon's Humvees eased to a stop several blocks from the mosque, allowing Crossman and five others to slip out and sneak toward the target. A row of abandoned houses across the street from the mosque would provide an ideal observation post, as long as the Soldiers could infiltrate undetected.

They moved into the house and set up with three Soldiers on one side of the abandoned house. The PL, interpreter, and the other Soldier were on the other side of the house, overwatching to the west.

Within a couple minutes, Crossman saw something alarming: young teenagers were walking around outside the mosque with AK-47s, a clear violation of the current weapons rules in the AO.

"Hey, these guys have AKs," he whispered over the radio.

"Yeah, I saw that," came the reply.

"Let's let the situation develop. See if there are some adults. Let's get more out of this."

The kids seemed to be patrolling around the mosque. They kept returning to a minivan parked on the side of the road.

The Friday prayer began—a rich, powerful voice emanating from the mosque. Crossman wondered why so many people were still out on the streets during the message.

The kids began walking directly toward Crossman's position. He looked at the terrain between his position and the mosque—a large fence stood in his path to the kids.

"Sir, what do you want to do, over?"

"Don't shoot," Crossman said. "I want to see who these kids are working with. Get ready to move."

Crossman readied a small foot patrol to chase the armed adolescents. He found a path out the building and around the fence toward the mosque.

By the time the patrol reached the mosque, the kids had disappeared.

"Where did they go?"

"I thought I saw them go into a building down that street," one Soldier said, pointing beyond the mosque.

"Me, too," said another.

"Let's go check it out," Crossman said.

A knock on the door yielded a throng of kids—ranging from grade-school-age to late teens—and they were all wearing the same color clothes as the armed teenagers.

"Can you believe this, sir? They all fucking look alike."

"Yeah, really weird," Crossman said.

"It's almost like they're trying to cover for them," an NCO said.

"Alright," Crossman said, "let's exfil."

30. CASEY BAKER

Lieutenant Casey Baker's trucks slithered along in the darkness, with a canal looming on each side of the muddy path.

"Ground guides."

A few of the leaders dismounted and sloshed through the mud in front of their trucks, ensuring the safe passage of their convoy.

The timeline was getting tight, and the entire squadron was waiting on Baker's unit. The trucks started bogging down. Their engines screaming, the trucks sunk deeper into the muck. Too much noise, and no progress. Now they had four trucks up to their axles in mud.

Baker's troop commander called for a SITREP on the radio. The hit time had been 0200. It was now almost 0300.

After coming to an opening between canals, one of the section sergeants noticed a possible short-cut across a field to a "hard-ball" road. The section sergeant approached Casey's platoon sergeant and made a recommendation to move to the road.

"No," the PSG said. "We stay off the hard-balls."

"Come on, Sergeant," the junior said, "it's time to use some common sense for once."

"No, we can make it from here."

"Yeah, this has been working out great. We've already missed our hit time."

"We STAY . . . OFF . . . the hard-balls."

"It'll take us forever!"

"I'm not fucking getting us blown up just to save a little *time*. There's fucking IEDs all around you, sergeant."

The NCOs were face-to-face in disagreement.

Tired, wet, and muddy, the section sergeant and platoon sergeant were about to get physical.

Casey got out of his vehicle and approached the angry NCOs. They ignored the PL and continued arguing face-to-face.

Lieutenant Baker utilized his best point of leverage to mediate the argument: the handle on the back of the body armor.

He grabbed his PSG's body armor and yanked him away from the section sergeant. With a few words, Casey abruptly re-focused their efforts on the blocking-position task, for which the entire Squadron was waiting.

The mission went off, late, yielding mediocre results—and a quiet, tired, and wet ride back to the FOB.

After closing on the base, the two NCOs bickered again before the section sergeant approached Casey for an immediate platoon reassignment.

"Sir, I'm serious," the NCO said. "I can't stand to work with him anymore. I want outta here."

"Shut the hell up and get some sleep," Casey told him. "We'll hash it out in the morning."

The next day, Casey could tell his platoon sergeant was pissed at him. After all, Casey had yanked around the highest-ranking NCO in the platoon by the handle on his body armor.

Both NCOs were sulking around the FOB, avoiding each other. Casey decided the rift had gone on too long. He called the two NCOs to his hooch to straighten it out.

"Now I know that mission a couple of nights ago was rough," Casey said. "It sucked for all of us. You think I like trudging through the mud trolling for IEDs? You think I like making the whole squadron wait on us to execute a raid? Look at you two. How long have you been together?"

"A long time, sir," the platoon sergeant answered. "Going on seven years."

"See, this is normal for guys like you to fight like this every once in a while. You're like brothers."

The NCOs glanced at each other without saying a word.

"Besides, you guys are NCOs," Casey said. "You have a responsibility to each other and to the unit to behave in a professional manner."

"Roger, sir," the platoon sergeant said. "I guess it was just a frustrating night, trying to get the convoy moving."

"I know," Casey said. "Believe me, I know."

He took a deep breath.

"So, you guys gonna be all right or what?"

"We'll be fine, sir," the section sergeant said. "No more problems."

"That's right," Casey said, nodding. "And don't forget who holds the ultimate power in the platoon." Casey started tapping his own chest. "I yanked you two apart like a couple of rag dolls."

The platoon sergeant cracked a smile, and then the three of them broke into laughter.

31. MARK HIEN

Lieutenant Mark Hien was walking out the front door of the house his platoon was clearing when muffled noises caught his attention. He turned and walked down a hallway towards the back of the house, where he heard a smacking sound coming from behind a closed door.

Opening the door, he saw one of his squad leaders punching a civilian in the head and stomach. At that moment, it reminded the PL of old film clips he'd watched of Joe Frazier punching Mohammed Ali when Ali had done his rope-a-dope routine. The Iraqi man was leaning back against a wall, crouching forward with his elbows held high to his ears to protect himself.

"Hey!" Mark yelled. "Cut that shit out!"

The NCO stopped immediately and looked at his platoon leader.

"Get in the truck, Sergeant," Mark told him. "You're done for today."

The platoon leader glared at the other Soldiers in the room, wordlessly expressing his anger and disappointment in them.

A team leader began to argue with the PL.

"Sir, you can just tell this guy's dirty."

"Maybe so," Mark cut him off, "but you blew it. Fucking leave him alone. Move out to the next house."

As his Soldiers filed out of the room past him, Hien told them, "We have a lot more houses to clear, and that will be the *last* time that happens."

32. JOHN ROGERS

Lieutenant John Rogers, a Stryker Infantry platoon leader, was enjoying a day of joint training with Iraqi Police from a local station. They were conducting weapons familiarization, with his Soldiers training the IP on the M4, and the IP training his guys on the AK-47. After that, they planned to train together on room-clearing techniques. Rogers saw the day as a fun way to build relationships with a group of local Iraqis who were crucial to gaining intelligence and fostering security in his unit's AO.

Everything changed when Rogers heard over the company net that 1st Platoon was in contact. A convoy of 30 HETs, each hauling an M1A2 tank, had been hit by an IED along the MSR through Baghdad. 1st Platoon had rushed to the convoy's aid, only to come under heavy small-arms fire. One of the transportation Soldiers had been shot, and 1st Platoon needed to evacuate the casualty. Rogers' platoon moved out swiftly to secure the now-stopped, 30-truck convoy that was stretched, or more precisely, dangerously gaggled, along a major highway with no nearby exits, under fire, in a built-up area of Baghdad. Four of the HETs were disabled.

Rogers' plan was to secure the site and dismount some of his Soldiers to drive the tanks off the disabled trucks and to a secure FOB. Some of his Soldiers, including his platoon sergeant, had previous experience with tanks. Upon arriving at the site, Rogers was shocked at the size of the convoy, which had no apparent leadership or organic security. The drivers and TCs were hiding inside their cabs. Rogers dismounted his team of tankers to figure things out on the ground, but they came under several volleys of small-arms fire and returned to the Strykers. One round smashed a blast plate inches in front of Rogers' face.

As Rogers attempted to positively identify the attackers and report the situation to Higher, HETs began to move along the road. The 26 trucks in the convoy that were mission capable resumed their convoy—without communicating with Rogers—leaving behind four damaged trucks, each with an M1A2 tank on its trailer. Perhaps the transportation unit had sent a message; Rogers couldn't be sure. The noise of the constant gunfire from his platoon's .50 cal and M240 machine guns and M4 rifles made it almost impossible for him to hear transmissions over the radio net.

The Iraqi Police sitting in the back of his Stryker weren't helping at all. They were screaming in fear, praying aloud, clearly wanting Rogers to take them out of their dangerous predicament. Rogers tried to calm them down, assuring them they were safe. He almost believed himself. Rogers received his first good news when one of his squads was able to identify and destroy an enemy fighting position in an apartment building. Yet, small-arms fire continued from several directions.

The battalion QRF, another Stryker platoon, arrived. This doubled Rogers' combat power. The QRF also provided several more tankers who joined the dismounted element. Rogers again sent the dismounted element out onto the trucks, where they had to mount each trailer, cut the tanks' locks, and insert a two-person crew into the turret and driver's compartments. The time on top of the vehicles exposed them to enemy fire. One of Rogers' Soldiers was shot in the back as he attempted to climb into a tank. Rogers' medic dismounted, and with the platoon sergeant on the ground began treatment and CASEVAC.

Rogers then got the call that the Air Weapons Team—attack aviation—was coming on station and awaiting his direction.

This is chaos, he thought. I'm under direct fire from several directions from positions we can't identify. Higher keeps calling and demands reports— IMMEDIATELY—about everything: the CASEVAC status, the number and names of the Iraqi Police we're carrying, the status on getting the tanks off, do I need more 19Ks? All I need is for them to get off my back and allow me to figure things out. I've got my platoon and the QRF platoon, a dismounted CASEVAC operation, a dismounted tank-starting operation—and one of the tanks has a dead battery—and now I'm supposed to manage an AWT!

Incoming mortar rounds began to fall. At this point, the tanks had been stranded for almost two hours in downtown Baghdad.

To Rogers' relief, 1st Platoon returned from its CASEVAC mission. He directed them to pick up the newest casualty and evacuate him back to the FOB.

Rogers then heard his battalion commander's voice on the net. It was music to his ears.

"Comanche Four-Six, this is Tomahawk Six. I'm inbound with the battalion TAC and a platoon from Apache company. How can we help you?"

"Tomahawk Six, if you control your element, the QRF, and the AWT, I'll handle local security and the tank-recovery operation," replied Rogers.

There were now 15 Strykers on station, and Tomahawk Six went on the offensive. The two platoons of Stryker Infantry began clearing the buildings on both sides of the highway. One Soldier identified an enemy forward observer talking on a cell phone. He shot and killed the man, and the enemy mortar fire ceased.

As the clearing operation progressed, enemy small-arms fire diminished. The tank-recovery team was able to move two tanks off their trailers. After using a slave cable to start the third tank, the Soldiers discovered that the ramp for the fourth tank was blocked by one of the disabled tractor-trailers. They moved that trailer and at last had all four tanks on the highway, manned by tankers.

The tanks did not have any radios or ammunition in them. Rogers provided each crew an MBITR and kept a Stryker close by, within radio range. He also ordered the tank crews to orient the main guns as if they had ammunition.

The convoy of Strykers and tanks moved to the safety of a FOB without further incident.

33. BEN MELTON

Lieutenant Ben Melton's platoon cordoned off the area around the girl's school. The last time he had secured this school for a visit, his platoon had stumbled across a seemingly harmless jumble of wire, typical for a construction site. But that assessment was proven wrong when the bomb attached to the wires exploded, taking a chunk of the schoolhouse with it. The platoon suffered no casualties that day, and Melton counted the result as a fortunate discovery of a new enemy tactic.

This time, anything out of the ordinary was cause for alarm, and the stakes were higher. Melton's battalion commander, sergeant major, an Iraqi city councilman, and their personal-security detachments were parked in the street as Melton's platoon investigated every inch of the building's exterior. His battalion commander was insistent on visiting the school. The commander exited his vehicle and started pacing in the street.

Melton persuaded his battalion commander back into his vehicle and surveyed the crowded battle space around him.

"Too many chiefs," Melton muttered under his breath, watching as security-detachment personnel wandered in the street. He noted how difficult it would be to coordinate a response if an attack occurred.

One of Melton's NCOs spotted a wire buried shallow in the dirt and run up the side of the outer walls and into the building. It appeared too professional to be an IED—like it was the work of an electrician. But Melton called EOD anyway.

The platoon watched and waited. EOD arrived and traced the wire through the building. They followed it through air ducts, electrical boxes, and under the floor.

EOD followed the wire from room to room, uncovering 155mm rounds and mixed explosives mere feet away from where Melton's platoon had been pulling security. In all, EOD uncovered nine IEDs: rigged propane tanks and 155mm rounds hidden in an air duct and buried under a long hallway floor.

Six hours later, the building was given the "all clear," but the planned walk-through of the new all-girls school had long since passed.

34. MURPHY WHITE

"Load 'em up on the trucks," bellowed Lieutenant Murphy White.

His Soldiers hoisted the blindfolded detainees onto the back of the Humvees. Murphy gave the signal to roll out and surveyed his convoy from his lead vehicle. As they started to move, he noticed the .50 cal in the truck behind him bouncing around errantly, as if not properly secured. White assumed that the driver and TC of the truck noticed it, too. He concluded that the mount must be busted and made note to check it later. He then turned his attention to other things.

When the convoy arrived at the FOB, White gave the order to unload the detainees. He noticed that one detainee had blood splattered on his blindfold. When he approached the detainee, a Soldier explained that the truck's .50 cal had swung around during the ride, repeatedly knocking the detainee in the head. White checked the mount. It wasn't broken, just unsecured.

White confronted the truck's driver about it. He knew his Soldiers secured their .50 cals instinctively; it had never been a problem before. He was curious that this should happen as detainees sat helpless and blindfolded in the back. The driver denied any responsibility, claiming it was all an accident.

MONTH FIVE

35. STEPHEN DUPERRE

Lieutenant Stephen DuPerre and his platoon convoyed through the streets of Baghdad on a sunny summer day. Children were playing along the street, which put the platoon leader at ease. This was a Shiite neighborhood where the local militia was careful to avoid causing collateral damage that killed other Shia.

BOOOM!

An IED exploded behind Steve's vehicle. His driver accelerated. Looking in his rear-view mirror, Steve saw the Humvee behind his appear safely through the cloud of dust.

DOH-DOH-DOH-DOH-DOH-DOH-DOH!

Steve ducked as the .50 caliber machinegun on his truck kicked into action. Just outside his bullet-proof window, he saw two AK-47-wielding men crumble to the ground barely 20 feet from his fast-moving truck.

As his platoon consolidated on the far side of the kill zone, the platoon leader asked his gunner what had happened.

"I saw two dudes coming out of the gate with AKs," the gunner said, "and I dropped them."

"Great shooting!" Steve said to his gunner. "Hell of a fast reaction. They didn't know what hit them!" Steve knew that the line between who lives and who dies in a firefight is a narrow one. His well-trained Soldiers had prevailed in today's contest!

After his platoon was consolidated and had sent up its reports, DuPerre led his Soldiers back down the street to secure the area for exploitation. Usually, crowds stayed away from Americans after an attack like this one. Not this time. As soon as he moved into the area, angry Iraqis approached him.

"What's the problem?" he asked his interpreter.

"They say that the two men we killed were not AIF," reported his terp. "They say the men were 'neighborhood watch.' They say the men rushed outside to help when they heard the explosion."

Later, on the subdued drive back to the FOB, the platoon leader's mind was on his gunner.

"You did the right thing today," DuPerre reassured the specialist. "I'm proud of you, I'm proud of how good a gunner you are, and if we're ever in the same situation, I hope to God you react the exact same way."

"Hooah, sir," replied his gunner.

36. JIM FREEZE

Speaking of the future, I'll share some thoughts that have come out as I've been pondering this war and talking it over with others. I'll tell you straight up that no one wants this war to be over more than the Soldiers who are over here. You will not find a single person here who would say they'd rather be deployed than back in the U.S. There is no question about it. At the same time, however, we also have a different perspective on the importance of winning this war. Not only is Iraq of strategic geographical significance; not only is freedom unconditionally superior to oppression; not only is American resilience and integrity on the line; but we should not quit just because it's tough.

To see the terror that this country faces daily is devastating. I sometimes wonder if it is really worth it, but then I think if our efforts prevent one attack from occurring in the US, then it's absolutely worth it. As much as I want to be home, I want a victory more because I don't want anything like I've seen here to reach the

U.S. So I thank you for your continued support because it goes so much farther than you know. It gives us strength and motivation to push on. On the other hand, I can also say from experience how demoralizing it can be to hear so many Americans demand that we withdraw. The message that sends to us is that what we're doing here is worthless; that we're not making a difference; that those who have given their lives fighting this war died for nothing. It also sends a message that America can be defeated, that we will surrender under pressure. Our Soldier's Creed forbids us to accept that. But then we see first hand in the eyes of a man holding his 2-year-old little girl telling us that he sleeps peacefully at night when Coalition Forces are nearby and it all comes back into perspective. Does this country have problems? More than you know. But we're part of the problem now and we're part of the solution as well. It will take time. Get the troops home safely as soon as possible, but get them home victoriously. Again, thank you all so much for your encouragement and support as we sweat our tails off over here.

37. BRIAN LARSON

"Collapse the cordon," Lieutenant Brian Larson ordered. Two Bradley Fighting Vehicles that had protected the platoon's eastern flank all day moved to link up with the vehicles on the western side of the cordon.

The day's cordon-and-search had been very successful. In the backyard of an unoccupied residence, Larson's platoon sergeant had initially found some buried 155-mm artillery rounds. Further digging by the platoon uncovered a cache that extended under the entire backyard: RPG launchers and rounds, fertilizer, wire, and blasting caps. The platoon had spent all day cataloguing and removing the cache, and now it was time to return to the FOB.

Larson and one of his squads were walking out to the street to link up with their Bradleys when a blue car sped in from the east and pulled into the house's driveway. Brian couldn't believe his eyes.

As the driver opened his door and began to exit his car, his eyes met Brian's. Both froze for a moment. Then the man jumped back into his car.

"Stop!" Larson yelled, signaling the same by raising and cupping his left hand. With his right arm, he raised his M4 and took aim. Brian had a clear shot through the windshield.

"Stop!" Larson repeated.

The man was unarmed. Larson knew they didn't have a target packet on him. Larson thought about the letter of admonishment he'd received for killing the old man at the TCP.

The Iraqi man started the engine, put it in reverse, ducked below the dashboard and accelerated back onto the street.

Larson opened fire. Several of his Soldiers did as well with their small arms. The car began to speed off down the street to the east. Larson and his Soldiers unleashed a fusillade of rounds into the car, but it escaped into the distance.

"Damn!" said the PL, looking to his Soldiers. "I should have shot him when I had the chance."

38. JARED OREN

Lieutenant Jared Oren was reading a book when one of his Soldiers burst into his office.

"Sir, the wood thieves are at it again!" he said.

Oren and his Soldier rushed outside in time to see an Army truck driving off across the FOB. They jumped into a Humvee and gave chase, catching up to it just as a SGT began to unload the booty of 4'x 8' plywood. Oren was pissed!

"What the FUCK do you think you are doing, Sergeant?" Oren yelled as he got into the NCO's face. "You think it's cool to steal another unit's property? We need this wood for our mission tomorrow."

The NCO didn't seem sufficiently scared, so Oren upped the ante.

"You ever heard of something called the UCMJ?" the LT asked.

"Easy now, Lieutenant," came a voice. It was the SGT's first sergeant.

"Don't 'easy' me, First Sergeant," Oren replied. "You're the one who's running a company of undisciplined criminals . . . ."

That's all it took. The 1SG exploded verbally on Oren, who answered in kind. At one point, they found themselves arguing about whose unit was more full of "faggots."

Their argument came to a quick halt when another voice entered the scene.

"What the hell are you doing in my company area, Lieutenant?" It was a captain, the first sergeant's company commander.

Without waiting for an answer, he told Oren, "I suggest you turn around, get in your truck, and never show your face in the First Sergeant's and my company area ever again."

Oren didn't want to leave without the stolen plywood, but could see that the CPT was not going to listen to anything he had to say. The argument with the company's 1SG had gotten personal, and the CPT was backing up his 1SG.

Oren turned and walked slowly away, wishing for a do-over.

39. BRITTANY MEEKS

"Lieutenant Meeks, we'll take the detainee from here," the major said. "There's a transpo convoy under heavy attack on MSR Tampa. We need you to get out there now!"

"Roger, sir," Lieutenant Brittany Meeks said. "Where abouts?"

"Near Checkpoint 38," he said.

"Got it sir," Meeks replied.

Meeks refocused her MP platoon for the next mission. The platoon turned around and rolled out the gate in its six Humvees.

Arriving at the scene of the attack, Meeks saw burning chassis of some 2½-ton trucks amid a gaggle of supply vehicles parked at odd angles on both sides of the road. Gunfire roared all around. Two AH-64s were zooming overhead and a lone Blackhawk helicopter was circling the area as if it were trying to land. It was a MEDEVAC bird.

"Suppress the enemy and secure that convoy," Meeks ordered her PLT. "We have to get that MEDEVAC on the ground."

Meeks' platoon quickly secured the convoy. Minutes later, Meeks was looking out the front of her Humvee when she saw one of the Apaches flash into a ball of flames. It spiraled downward into a nearby neighborhood.

"Bird down, bird down, bird down!" Meeks called over the net.

She alerted her platoon to move. They rolled to the crash site and secured the area.

The platoon had trained on similar scenarios prior to the deployment. Meeks sent out search teams to the buildings around the crash site, ordering them to clear house-to-house.

The Apache was burning in the field nearby. Its ammunition started cooking off. Meeks and her platoon couldn't get close to the wreckage, much less recover the aircrew.

Meeks's brigade commander rolled up with his personal security detachment. He headed straight for the platoon leader.

"Lieutenant Meeks, how come every time I see you, things are blowing up?" he said.

"I don't know, sir," she said.

"How can I help?" he asked.

"Sir, what I really need you guys to do is take your PSD and trucks and fill in security on this part of our perimeter," Meeks said, pointing. "I also need your guys to search those abandoned vehicles to our flank."

"Got it," he said.

The brigade commander turned and strode back to his vehicles, and within a few seconds, he and his PSD were searching vehicles and securing the flank of Brittany's platoon.

40. DOUG BOLDWIN

In the back of his mind, Lieutenant Doug Boldwin was thinking: *this is wrong, I could get in trouble for this.*

But this was war, and in this environment, Boldwin followed his heart and his gut instinct. When he hit the wrong house, he could still make good use out of it by getting enough intel to move to another target.

Boldwin knew something bad had been going down in this neighborhood, but he didn't know how to prove it. With no physical evidence, all he had were detainees. And so he used them.

He contemplated how he should handle each detainee.

Do I scare this guy? Coerce him? Offer him money?

71

The previous time, Doug had given a guy $60 for some information but had gotten totally fooled. The info was completely false.

So this time he decided to use other means. He was pretty sure he was only allowed to ask his detainees the "Five W's," but he needed more than that. The Army expected him to turn his detainees over to a Tactical HUMINT Team, a team that was rarely in the area, didn't know the people, and wouldn't have to deal with the repercussions of a tough interrogation.

So Boldwin rationalized it to himself.

It's not what the Army would say is right, but I know not to cross that line. I know how far is too far. I'm not going to cripple anybody or kill anybody; but I'll do what I have to in order to scare someone if it's gonna save a Soldier's life in the future.

So he handled it himself, not wanting to put his Soldiers at risk. Boldwin and his interpreter used their standard practice: take the detainee into a dark bathroom, turn out the lights, and scare the hell out of him. Boldwin knew he wasn't supposed to do it. But everyone did it, and everyone *knew* everyone was doing it. They all just gave the *nod, nod, wink, wink.*

And almost every time it paid off.

But when does it go too far? Boldwin asked himself.

He comforted himself with a familiar answer: *I can't define it, but I'll know it when I see it.*

41. CHRIS CROFFORD

As the raid came to a close, Lieutenant Chris Crofford moved to the front seat of his Humvee to begin completing the mound of paperwork necessary for processing his new detainees. His platoon was still in the house, finishing the search and trying to return the residence to normal.

His platoon had so many detainees that Crofford's sister platoon was ordered in to backhaul them.

The other platoon arrived and jumped into action, joining his platoon in the target house. After a few minutes, Crofford was briefly distracted from his forms by yelling and loud noises, which seemed to be coming from the vicinity of his sister platoon, which had already started moving detainees to their vehicles. It sounded like they were getting rough with the detainees. Crofford knew if he stopped to go investigate, it would only prolong everyone's time on the objective. So he ignored the raucous in the interest of time.

Back on the FOB, Crofford couldn't stop thinking about the possible mistreatment of detainees from his raid. He resolved to overcome his own excuses for inaction and his fears of a backlash from his peers. He sought out his commander and reported the incident.

42. CHRIS FORD

Lieutenant Chris Ford walked over to his National Police counterpart on their joint patrol.

"The men are clean," Ford told him, referring to two men that the patrol had stopped to question. "We have nothing on them. Release them."

The NP lieutenant refused to release them.

"Our joint patrol is over," he told Ford. "You can go now."

Chris felt uncomfortable with the situation. He asked his company's IO officer, a fellow lieutenant who had accompanied him on the patrol, to mingle with the lower-ranking NPs to figure out what was going on.

Chris looked over at the BBC film crew that was accompanying the uneventful patrol.

Ford's interpreter returned from his own reconnaissance, out of breath.

"I just overhead," he said, "the NP Lieutenant telling those two men that this would be their last day alive. They are Sunni." Ford knew that the National Police unit was entirely Shia.

"Change of mission," Ford informed the small group of American Soldiers who were with him on the ground. "Protect these men."

The Americans formed a circle, standing shoulder-to-shoulder around the two men, facing out.

Seeing this, the NP lieutenant flew into a rage and began barking orders.

The National Police Humvees that formed the patrol's inner cordon re-oriented their weapons inward and took aim at Ford and his Soldiers. National Policemen on the ground, who outnumbered the Americans, encircled Ford's Soldiers. One National Policeman shoved the barrel of his AK-47 into the cheek of one of Ford's men.

The Soldier, in turn, pressed the barrel of his shotgun into the Iraqi's face.

Ford's interpreter leaned over to him.

"The Lieutenant just ordered his men to open fire on us if we don't turn over these men, who he's calling 'terrorists,'" the interpreter said.

Ford radioed a SITREP to his platoon sergeant, who was located with all the platoon's vehicles on an outer cordon. Within seconds, Ford's gun trucks encircled the Iraqi gun trucks, weapons trained on the National Police.

Ford reviewed the situation. Behind him stood two innocent men. Shoulder-to-shoulder with him stood a small group of his lightly armed Soldiers. In front of him were two concentric circles of National Police who had received conditional orders to open fire on him and his men. On the outermost ring, Ford saw his own gun trucks and his very pissed-off platoon sergeant.

The only people there who didn't appear disturbed were the BBC film crew capturing the drama.

"Don't point your weapons at the NPs," Ford ordered his platoon in as calm and even a voice as he could muster. His Soldiers complied; the one Soldier lowered his shotgun.

Ford attempted to reason with his counterpart, but the NP officer remained agitated and determined to take control of the two Sunni men. The National Police platoon's liaison to American forces tried to negotiate, but the NP lieutenant held his position.

"Lieutenant Ford," announced loudly the IO officer. "I just heard from Brigade. It turns out that these two men are on the HVT list. The brigade commander says we have to take them to the BHA for interrogation."

His fellow lieutenant didn't outright say, "hint, hint, wink, wink," but Ford got the message.

They both knew that Iraqis respect and fear higher-ranking authorities. The NP lieutenant would understand that Ford had no option except to obey such a senior commander, and that there would be no shame in him now allowing the Americans to keep the Sunnis.

Ford informed the National Police lieutenant of the situation, ordered his Soldiers to "detain" the two men, and immediately moved with his Soldiers and their detainees through the rings of NPs to their vehicles.

The platoon moved out as quickly as possible. On the way back to the FOB, Ford took a moment to thank his fellow lieutenant.

"Quick thinking out there," he said. "That situation almost got out of hand."

43. GAVIN HADDUCK

Lieutenant Gavin Hadduck and his platoon moved dismounted out of their company combat outpost and into the adjacent village. The people there were not friendly. Gavin's company had moved into the area a month before and was hard at work "winning hearts and minds."

For weeks they had been handing out teddy bears and school supplies and waving at people—people who in response glared back at them with disdain. One little boy had even refused a candy bar from one of his Soldiers. What kind of child refuses chocolate?

Hadduck didn't agree with his battalion's approach. He had joined the Army after 9-11 in order to kill the enemies of his country, not to pretend to like people who supported the enemy. But Hadduck was a good Soldier and was trying his best to win *the Petraeus way*.

The patrol moved off the hardtop road into the lush green vegetation of the village along the Euphrates River. They passed some locals who were walking the other way. The troops were halfway across the field of knee-high grass when BOOM! an explosion blew Hadduck onto the ground ten feet away.

Regaining his senses, Hadduck moved to the blast site. He passed some equipment and a dazed Iraqi Army soldier whose arm was hanging by threads of flesh and moved to his stricken Soldier, who was lying on his back, both legs sheared off.

The platoon medic was on the scene in a heartbeat, placing tourniquets on the bleeding stumps and assuring the still-conscious Soldier that he would be okay.

Hadduck assessed the situation. Security looked to be in place. MEDEVAC . . . not. His platoon sergeant and RTO were frozen, mesmerized, horrified. Hadduck ran to his RTO, grabbed the hand mike, reported the situation and requested a MEDEVAC. Then he noticed what his PSG and RTO were staring at. That "equipment" Hadduck had seen after the blast . . . was the remains of one of his Soldiers.

Hadduck returned to his wounded Soldier, who had lost consciousness. He performed mouth-to-mouth resuscitation while his medic massaged his heart, but it was futile. The injuries were too extensive. Gavin Hadduck's Soldier died in front of his eyes.

Later, talking with his platoon sergeant in their platoon bay, Hadduck seethed with anger.

"Those villagers knew that IED was in the field," he said. "They let us walk right past it to our deaths. We renovate their school, and what do we get? Two dead brothers."

On their subsequent patrols, Hadduck's Soldiers turned up the heat.

"It's 'game on,'" he instructed his Soldiers. "They want a war, they'll get one."

His Soldiers no longer knocked on doors; they kicked them down. They didn't carefully replace items in houses during searches; they tossed them. On a few occasions it looked to Hadduck that his Soldiers were about to lose control. He reeled them in.

Hadduck wouldn't tolerate any beatings of detainees or wrongful killings, and his Soldiers knew that. It's not that he and his

Soldiers didn't feel like killing everyone in the village; they did. But their reason prevailed over their emotions.

"At some point," Hadduck explained to his Soldiers, "this deployment will be over, and I want us all to be able to get on with our lives, not be stuck in jail. We'll leave this country with our honor intact."

MONTH SIX

44. JOHN DOLAN

Lieutenant John Dolan took his position in the lead boat. His platoon had trained in the gunboats only once before.

Their mission was to recon possible river landing points and to monitor Friday prayer at a local mosque—from a flotilla of four Iraqi-piloted, American-led gunboats.

The task was a stretch for the platoon, but was no surprise, given the theme of the whole deployment thus far: ever-changing, uncertain, ambiguous, volatile. Even the way the day had started, under dark skies and a heavy rain, were conditions that Dolan had never expected to face in "barren, desert Iraq."

As soon as Dolan ordered the boats into the water, the rain stopped.

The boats began cruising southward down the Tigris River at a comfortable pace. After about three kilometers, they were sprinkled with light small-arms fire from somewhere along the bank. The platoon powered on, mission-focused.

The gunfire picked up.

Dolan began weighing his mission objective versus the amount of fire his boats were taking. He realized that they couldn't sustain small-arms fire for long in the boats, and it occurred to him it would be much easier to accomplish the mission on land in their Bradleys.

"Turn the boats around!" he said.

The command echoed across the radio in familiar voices. As their convoy slowed and circled, the firing stopped. The next kilometer back up the river was clear.

The patrol was about two kilometers from their start point when a deluge of bullets hit. Waves of gunfire poured from the banks of the river. People streamed out of their houses, shooting at the passing boats.

"Punch it! Get us out of here!" he said.

The boats surged ahead at full throttle, nearing 50 miles per hour.

Dolan noticed a distinct popping sound just before he was hit.

SMACK!

A tiny lead shard ripped through his elbow and triceps. Another round slashed across his ribs.

The pain was blunt and heavy, like being hit with a sledgehammer. Then his arm and ribs went numb.

Dolan realized that several men in his boat were hit. The Iraqi coxswain was slumped over the boat's steering controls, veering the boat hard right.

The boat slammed into an island in the middle of the river.

For the next several minutes, Dolan fought with his team to secure their crash site. The Soldiers in two of the platoon's four boats continued northward to base.

The NCO in the boat closest to Dolan's noticed his platoon leader's boat crashed on the island.

"Turn around!" he said. "The PL's boat just crashed!"

As the NCO's boat turned, it became stuck on a sand bar in the middle of the river. Soldiers jumped out of the boat to dislodge it. When the boat returned to float, the engines were damaged from the crash. The men were stuck on the sandbar and taking fire.

"Get to the shore!" ordered the NCO.

The team scurried off the sandbar and into the river, fighting to find some cover.

Meanwhile, Dolan huddled under the grounded and now-sideways steel boat, with river reeds and grasses partially obscuring his men's position. Bullets whizzed overhead and *tinked* against the hull as the medic applied a pressure dressing to Dolan's arm.

Of the ten men hunkering around the crash boat, four were wounded. An NCO ordered the men into a small perimeter. The island sat like a stage in the middle of the river, with thirty-foot cliffs on some sides.

Dolan noticed they had landed right in front of a mosque on the bank of the river. They could hear a voice on a loud speaker, an eerie singing in Arabic. It wasn't the mosque they had been tasked to monitor, but at least they were monitoring a mosque.

"What's he saying?" Dolan asked his interpreter.

"He is telling the people to come out and fight the Americans," he said.

It was a call to arms, as if the town itself was moving in to overtake Dolan's position in the middle of the river.

Dolan grabbed the radio to call in support from the other boats. He couldn't get comms. Dolan low-crawled to the NCO's position.

"Sergeant, we can't stay here," Dolan said. "Destroy the boat," Dolan said. "Let's get ready to go."

"Sir, we're getting low on ammo."

Dolan began to move and his team fell in behind him. As they ran across the island, Dolan could feel the adrenaline kicking in. Blood started to pour out of his wound.

They moved about 100 meters north on the island in order to prepare for an air extraction. When he stopped moving, Dolan started to feel dizzy. He looked down and saw his arm soaked in blood and a steady red flowed pumping from his wound. He called the medic.

"Doc, I think you should check this out," Dolan said.

"Yeah, sir, you need a tourniquet on that," the medic said.

Dolan readied his weapon in his right hand and eyed a possible LZ for air extraction.

On the radio, he established comms with attack helicopters.

"Crazyhorse, my four boats, my element has been split. We are cut off. Surrounded. They have overwhelmed us. We are surrounded by 70 or so insurgents on both sides of the river . . . ."

The Apaches came in hot, pouring withering fire onto the riverbanks that diminished the enemy fire. The situation stabilized.

Air extraction was coordinated. One of Dolan's Soldiers popped yellow smoke, and an hour after crashing onto the island, Dolan's team loaded onto two Blackhawk helicopters and returned to base.

45. MATT MARTINEZ

"Six, looks like we've got a possible dead body in the street, over."

"Roger," Lieutenant Matt Martinez said. "Proceed with caution."

When Martinez's men moved closer, they discovered that the man was still alive, with a gunshot wound that had entered through his mouth and exited out the back of his neck. The man was still breathing and able to talk.

"Need the interpreter over here. This man's still alive."

Martinez and his interpreter approached the wounded man. The man told the Soldiers he had been carjacked.

Martinez looked around and saw throngs of people in the neighborhood going about their business, ignoring the wounded man who was lying in a gutter full of trash with flies gathering on him.

Martinez got on the radio and called back to his FOB to request an Iraqi Army ambulance.

"Is he Iraqi Army?" came the reply.

"No."

"Wait, over."

A few minutes later, he got an answer to his request.

"The IA won't send an ambulance unless he's IA."

"Okay," Martinez said. "Well, can I bring him to our aid station there?"

"We're not sure if we can treat him unless he was working for Coalition Forces or he was wounded by Coalition Forces. The best thing you can do is take him to a local hospital in the area."

Martinez didn't have an easy way to contact the hospital. The only hospital in the vicinity that had the resources to treat such a severe injury was located in a Shia area. Martinez was currently in a Sunni neighborhood. He looked around and began asking people standing around to help.

No one would help him.

Martinez called his Humvee forward and loaded the bleeding man in the back seat with his interpreter. Martinez jumped back into his truck and keyed the hand mike.

"All right," Martinez said, "let's get this guy to a hospital."

46. PATRICK HENSON

Lieutenant Patrick Henson wasn't sure if he should feel guilt, pity, or anger. He felt some of each.

There he stood in the living room of an Iraqi family amid the non-stop sounds of wailing by a woman and her four children. He had never heard people cry so relentlessly loudly, and it was really getting on his nerves. They had been carrying on like this for more than an hour, ever since Henson and his platoon had arrived to detain the HVI who was their husband and father.

The platoon had not yet taken the man because they first needed to find a particular cell phone—one that linked the HVI to incriminating SIGINT.

When Henson had entered the house, he had asked the man and his wife if they had any cell phones.

"No, none," both had replied.

Since then, Henson's Soldiers had found four cell phones—hidden everywhere from inside a bathroom pipe to inside a woman's undergarments. But they had not found the particular cell phone they needed to arrest the man, who sat on the living room couch defiantly watching the Soldiers upend his house.

Henson had an idea. He signaled for the man to stand up. Soldiers inspected the couch, flipping it upside down in their increasingly desperate search for the cell phone.

"Got something," one announced. He held up a part of a cell phone.

The Soldiers then ripped into the couch, finding the other half of the phone in a separate section of it.

A squad leader re-assembled the parts, turned the phone on, and checked its phone number.

"Nice work, Sergeant," Henson said. "We found our guy."

As Henson's Soldiers led the zip-stripped man out of his house, the wailing sounds became even more shrill. But Henson didn't feel guilty anymore—just anger at the woman and pity for the children.

47. SCHUYLER WILLIAMSON

Schuyler Williamson and his platoon of three up-armored Humvees had just finished a six-hour patrol. They were parking their trucks in their company's combat outpost in Baghdad when they heard small-arms fire. It sounded to be less than a kilometer away, to the south.

Williamson's Soldiers continued recovering from their mission. The small-arms fire, however, didn't fade away as it usually did. Instead, the staccato sounds of automatic weapons continued, increasing in intensity. The heavy DOH-DOH-DOH-DOH of .50-caliber machine guns joined the chorus. Someone was in a serious firefight.

Williamson and his NCOs went to the outpost's command post to find out who was in contact. Neither his company nor battalion had any information on the incident. Williamson figured that the unit in contact must be an American patrol passing through his AO.

As the sounds of explosions joined the continuing small-arms fire, Williamson and his NCOs looked at each other and knew what had to be done. "Let's do it," he said. His NCOs yelled to their Soldiers, some of whom had already removed their battle rattle and were resting on their bunks. The Soldiers ran to their vehicles like firemen, excited at the prospect of joining a firefight.

Approximately 400 meters out the gate, Williamson saw the battle unfolding before him. A platoon of four Strykers was stopped on line on an east-west highway, engaging several enemy positions in a four-story building to their south. Concrete barriers erected by Americans to protect the neighborhood blocked the Strykers from maneuvering on the building. It appeared to Williamson that one Stryker vehicle was attempting to maneuver to a gap in the barriers to the east of the building, but withering enemy fire prevented its Soldiers from dismounting.

Williamson brought his platoon on line with the Strykers, tying into their western flank. He still did not have communications with the Stryker platoon. His three gunners unleashed their M240s into the fray, reducing the volume of fire coming from the bunkered enemy positions.

Williamson kept an eye on the easternmost Stryker vehicle. He wanted to be sure to know if American dismounts moved on the enemy positions.

BHOM! BHOM! BHOM! BHOM!

Four RPGs exploded near his platoon—narrowly missing the trucks, flattening several tires.

Enemy forces were firing on his platoon's right flank from the third floor of an apartment building to the west.

Williamson directed his platoon to shift their fires to this new enemy position. His platoon's medium machineguns were accurate but not able to stop the enemy fire.

"Give me a 203!" called Williamson's gunner, ducking down from his armored cupola. A Soldier in the back seat of the truck handed his grenade launcher to the gunner. On his first shot, the gunner placed a 40mm high-explosive grenade into the enemy position. The resulting explosion was disproportionately huge as it detonated an enemy cache. Enemy activity from that building ceased immediately.

Just as Williamson began to shift his focus back to the initial enemy positions, his battalion TOC radioed to him the unit and call sign of the Stryker platoon. Williamson cued up their radio net.

"Apache, this is Copper One, tied in to your west. SITREP, over."

"We are beginning to clear the objective, from west to east. If you could set up an outer cordon, that would be great," came the response from his fellow platoon leader.

Williamson set his trucks to block traffic coming from the west, north, and east, one Humvee covering each avenue of approach. Gaggles of Iraqi vehicles lined up in each direction. One white sedan, however, did not follow the crowd. It sped towards Williamson's vehicle from the north. Williamson's driver went through his escalation-of-force procedures, signaling the driver to stop and turn around, which he finally did.

Several minutes later, *the same vehicle* sped toward the platoon's eastern position. The Humvee gunner there signaled repeatedly for the approaching vehicle to stop, but it didn't. The gunner fired several warning shots, but still the speeding vehicle did not slow. The gunner engaged the car with several bursts from his M240. The car rolled to a halt, its engine smoking, its windshield shattered.

48. DEREK SYED

Lieutenant Derrick Syed parked his Humvee directly behind the Iraqi Police pick-up truck and walked up to the driver's side door. Traffic rumbled through this bustling five-way intersection one block outside of Sadr City. Syed wondered if these Sadr City police would ever learn to follow his guidance: *stay in your sector.*

Syed had a brief conversation with the IP who was at the wheel of the truck. It wasn't an overly polite discussion, as this was becoming an all-too-familiar occurrence.

"Okay," Syed concluded, "have a nice day. Move along now."

Syed turned to walk away and get on with his patrol when *WHAM*, something slammed into his shoulder—it felt like a big rock. He went down. His first impulse: *shoot the cops.*

The Iraqi Police laughed out loud as Syed struggled to get up, blood pouring from his shoulder. Syed scanned for targets. His platoon sergeant rushed out and pulled him behind cover. Syed had been shot by a sniper.

49. ZACH COOLEY

Lieutenant Zach Cooley's platoon was clearing the house of a known enemy sniper. Again. They had been to this house a month earlier but had been unable to find any evidence to help locate the infamous insurgent. Since then, the sniper was thought to have killed two more Americans.

The sniper's family members coldly watched Zach's Soldiers search their house.

An NCO approached his PL.

"Sir," said to Zach, "We can't find anything, but these people are bad. Why don't we do a quick "level-4" search before we head out of here?" In other words, he wanted to trash the place, leaving it in shambles.

Zach thought about it. It would feel real good—and would get some payback for his fallen comrades—to inflict a little pain on the family of the guy who had hurt so many American families.

"We can't do that, Sergeant," he replied. "We're the good guys, remember? We don't smash people's shit. You know, sometimes it sucks to be the good guys in a war."

A few minutes later, as the platoon prepared to end its search, the NCO again approached his PL. He held a key ring in his outstretched hand.

"Sir," he said, "it sure would suck for a family to lose all the keys to its locks. It might make it suck for them to be the bad guys in a war."

Zach thought about it. This option avoided the potential problems that trashing a house would have had.

"Good idea," he said. "Collect up all their keys."

As the platoon crossed over a bridge along its route back to the FOB, keys flew from the Humvees into the river below.

50. LAURA WEIMER

Lieutenant Laura Weimer sat in the backseat of a Humvee parked outside a DFAC, agonizing over whether to say something.

The pre-dawn darkness was silent except for occasional chatter on the radio net and intermittent snoring by the Soldier seated next to her. Inside her head, though, raged a loud debate.

Five hours before, Laura had been enjoying midnight chow in this DFAC when she ran into one of her squads taking a break from their 10-hour overnight patrol. Seeing her, the squad leader had enthusiastically invited her to join the squad for the remainder of the patrol.

Weimer had jumped at the opportunity. She was the new platoon leader, in her first week on the job. Her predecessor had been very popular, very competent. The platoon had excelled so far in the deployment, prevailing in firefights and earning widespread admiration. As the platoon's new leader, fresh from OBC and a few months on staff, Laura was anxious to log as much time outside the wire as she could.

The patrol had gone well—until the squad returned to the FOB at 0500 and parked outside the DFAC, waiting for it to open at 0600. Weimer *knew* that the patrol was supposed to last until 0600. She had delivered the patrol schedule. And so her inner debate raged on:

Should I say something? There's a reason the patrol is supposed to last until 0600—to keep coverage in sector. Do all the squads cut corners like this? Is this the unwritten norm? Or am I being tested? Everything I've ever read and heard is telling me to get the squad back out on patrol—that standards are standards. Maybe I'm being too "by the letter of the tasking," bringing a "staff" attitude to a platoon that has logged hundreds of hours on patrols. In the big picture, after all, what does it really matter if they hang out here for an hour? I wish I'd said something right away. With every minute here, it makes less sense to go back outside the wire. But with every minute here, I'm giving my seal of approval to this. And it feels wrong! But if speak up and I'm wrong, if this IS the standard, then I've just gotten off to a real bad start with the platoon; everyone will be mad at me. This would be the last time I'm ever invited on an extra patrol. Is this really a fight worth fighting?

The clanging of humvee doors rescued Laura from her internal dialogue, bringing a sense of relief. The patrol was over. 0600. Time for chow.

Yet the new platoon leader's second guessing was just beginning.

51. SHAWN JOKINEN

Lieutenant Shawn Jokinen finally went to bed at about 0530 after spending the whole night interrogating the leading suspects in the sniper killing of one of his youngest Soldiers, Private Paton.

An hour after bedding down, Jokinen was awoken by the Sergeant of the Guard.

"Sir, we're receiving small-arms fire from multiple directions," the NCO said. "And it's getting heavy."

Jokinen jumped out of bed. He could hear the rounds impacting the side of the building. An RPG ripped into a perimeter fighting position.

The PL began moving to his CP.

As he was about to enter the CP, he saw a large white cargo truck smash through the patrol base's front gate.

Shawn raised his rifle and began pumping rounds into the cab. The driver slumped over the wheel and the truck veered to the left and stopped.

Jokinen ran back into the building to get his body armor and helmet. When he got to the CP, he saw the Sergeant of the Guard there . . . .

CRA—RUMP!

A massive explosion decimated half the patrol base, flattening walls, tearing through the platoon's vehicles, and launching shrapnel throughout.

The CP's front wall blew in, burying Jokinen alongside the Sergeant of the Guard. The NCO was crushed. Jokinen clawed for air from beneath the pile of rubble.

Dazed, Jokinen pulled himself from the rubble and began directing his available shooters to defend against the attack as he administered buddy aid to those around him.

The white truck had been filled with explosives and used as a vehicle-borne IED. Out of 19 men on the patrol base in Tarmiyah, 17 were wounded or dead.

52. MATT BURCH

The boom echoed across the FOB. It was a huge blast, in the direction of Tarmiyah, several kilometers away. Lieutenant Matt Burch looked at his Soldiers and NCOs, but he didn't have to give any command—the reverberating sound cued his guys to gear up.

His Soldiers double—and triple-checked their equipment, and when the order came from Higher, they were loaded up and ready to go. The men were anxious to fight, especially after losing a friend, Paton, to sniper fire two days prior. Following a Bradley and a tank, they rolled in their Humvees towards first platoon's outpost.

The next call came just a few hundred meters from the FOB:

"Red One, Bandog Six, stand down, stay in place."

Burch was furious. He responded through clenched teeth: "We're already outside of the FOB. We're on our way."

"Red One, Bandog Six, I say again, stand down, stay exactly where you are."

"Roger."

Burch radioed his TCs: "Stop right here. The armor is going but we're staying right here."

The platoon halted and watched the armored vehicles drive out of sight to aid their brothers. The idling of Humvees provided a numbing backdrop to the thoughts of what they were missing.

Burch's driver swore and beat his fists. Burch heard some chatter on his radio: *Three KIA so far.* On his platoon net his Soldiers were cursing, demanding they be let out to help. They would give anything to help, to feel like part of the fight. Burch sensed this, felt the gravity of this moment in the mental health of his Soldiers. He needed to channel them on something.

"Block the road," Burch said. "Not a single person comes in or out. Snap TCP. Nobody in or out until they're done."

Burch knew they weren't going to make the firefight, but this would help. It would focus his Soldiers on something besides the battle they weren't going to be a part of and the comrades they weren't going to assist.

Burch heard of more casualties on the radio. He suppressed his sadness and decided not to tell his guys yet.

They got the order to return to the FOB. As soon as his truck rolled through the gate, Burch headed to the TOC to confirm the names of the casualties.

Then he summoned his platoon.

Burch had prepared grand rhetoric of sacrifice and honor in the back of his mind until he saw the looks on his men's faces, countenances he recognized from two nights earlier when they had lost a brother to the sniper's bullet.

Burch told them the names of the deceased and those who were wounded, but he didn't pretend to know the extent of their injuries or who among them would make it back. After his announcement, some of his men faded into their own corners; others beat their fists and threw things. Matt let them release their emotions here—lest they should find their outlet outside the wire.

MONTH SEVEN

53. STEVE LEDROIUX

"Sir, there they are again," said the Humvee driver on the intercom. An illegal checkpoint of the Mahdi Army blocked the Baghdad side street. This was the fourth time that LT Steve LeDroiux's platoon had seen a checkpoint there. On the three previous occasions, the militiamen had scattered into the urban jungle when the American patrol approached, and LeDroiux had always decided to continue on with his civil-affairs mission.

Today, LeDroiux was leading his patrol back from delivering supplies to a health clinic. Today he decided to address the illegal-checkpoint problem.

"Action on them," he ordered his platoon. "Let's detain one of them and see what we can get."

His Soldiers moved on the checkpoint. They followed one of the fleeing young men into a building and were able to detain him without incident. He was a teenage boy, wearing jeans and a white shirt instead of the typical black attire of the Mahdi militia. He was unarmed. LeDroiux knew they had nothing on him. They had not witnessed him actually participating in stopping any vehicles.

LeDroiux began to tactically question him. He knew that he couldn't threaten the detainee with bodily harm, but the lieutenant had become adept at asking the same questions in multiple ways to figure out if someone was lying. And those he questioned were usually lying.

"Where do you live?" LeDroiux asked.

"Not around here," said the boy.

"Who were those other people at the checkpoint?"

"I don't know anyone here. I was just passing by when your vehicles approached. The militiamen ran, so I did, too. But I'm not part of any militia and I don't know who any of them are."

LeDroiux knew in his gut that the kid was lying. He decided to call his bluff.

"Tell him that we're taking him to jail," he told his translator.

As the Americans put their blindfolded detainee into a Humvee, the Iraqi panicked.

"I must get my jacket from my friend!"

LeDroiux didn't know why the jacket was important to the boy, but he did now have evidence that the boy knew someone in the area. Thinking that the "friend" must also have been involved in the checkpoint, LeDroiux removed the blindfold and permitted the boy to walk to his friend's house, about 100 meters down the street.

Once the boy identified the house to the Americans, the Soldiers once again blindfolded him and put him in a Humvee.

"Don't worry. We'll get your jacket for you . . . and your friend."

LeDroiux's Soldiers cordoned the house and moved into it. They found nothing—no jacket, no person.

"Sir," one of his squad leaders said. "The kid out in the Humvee doesn't know that his friend wasn't here." The platoon leader, squad leader, and the two attached Iraqi translators quickly hatched a plan to get their detainee to talk. One of the two Iraqi translators would pretend to be the "captured friend."

The Soldiers slammed doors to simulate a violent capture and yelled at their fake "detainee" from inside the house, telling him that he better talk immediately unless he wanted to go to jail. They told him, loudly and translated into Arabic, that they didn't want "little fish" like him and the boy. They wanted information on "big fish" of the Mahdi Army. They informed their role-playing translator that they would release whoever gave them better information—him or the boy who had already "ratted him out" by leading the Americans to him.

The translator pretending to be a detainee agreed loudly to inform the Americans about anything they needed to know, as long as he was freed and his snitch of a friend back in the Humvee was jailed.

"I will tell you anything you want to know," he said in Arabic. "That dog can rot in your prison."

Overhearing this conversation from the back of an American Humvee, the blindfolded detainee was seized with fear. Anxious to be more cooperative than the sham detainee, he blurted out the name and location of a Mahdi Army member.

"You win, for now," LeDroiux told the boy, as his Soldiers mounted their vehicles to move to the new location. "Let's see if you're telling the truth." When the platoon approached the target house, they removed the detainee's blindfold so he could positively identify the house.

"That's the one," said the boy, and the blindfolds were put back over his eyes.

"Let's take it," LeDroiux ordered his men.

This time, they found the man they were looking for, who had an AK-47 but did not resist. The Soldiers disarmed and blindfolded their new detainee, their bigger fish.

This time, the translator posing as a detainee remained outside the house, so the new detainee could not see him. LeDroiux offered his new detainee the same deal—lead the way to a bigger fish or go to jail. They told him about their "other detainee." The role-playing translator outside loudly expressed his willingness to cooperate for his freedom. Fearful of detention, the new detainee blurted out the location of a Mahdi Army safehouse.

"This better be worth it," LeDroiux told his most recent detainee as his platoon quickly moved out to the new location. Repeating his successful TTP, LeDroiux had his detainee positively identify the location.

His men moved into position and conducted a hasty raid on the house. This time, they hit paydirt—four Mahdi personnel with uniforms and a cache of AK-47s, pistols, and bomb-making materials. Some big fish. LeDroiux's Soldiers exploited the site and successfully handed these four detainees and their evidence over for detention in the Division Holding Area.

As he had promised them, LeDroiux released his first two detainees, the little fish who had cooperated.

54. ELIZABETH ZERWICK

Lieutenant Elizabeth Zerwick stood at a massive table heaped with rice and lamb and fish and chicken and bread. She was one of about 20 people standing around the table, but she was the only woman there.

The Iraqis were digging in—grabbing fists full of rice and tearing meat off the bone, mixing it up in their grips. The eating seemed as simple as it gets, but Elizabeth still had trouble adjusting.

On a normal day, Elizabeth's platoon would visit the police stations, conduct joint patrols, interact with the locals, set up checkpoints, and train the Iraqi Police on basic tasks.

It was not unusual for men in Iraq to treat her differently. Elizabeth had already received several marriage proposals from Iraqi men she worked with.

But today, Elizabeth was the guest of honor of the Iraqi Police district commander, who had invited Iraqi Army leaders, local religious and tribal leaders, his station commanders, and other district commanders. Not only was she the only female there, she was by far the lowest-ranking person there—relatively speaking.

She viewed the occasion as a validation of her approach thus far: *I'm not here to take over your operation. I respect your culture. I just want to learn from you and teach you what I know, so the Iraqi people can live more securely.*

55. JED POMFRET

Lieutenant Jed Pomfret and his platoon moved through the dark streets of Baghdad on their way to an Iraqi Police station.

Pomfret's platoon was responsible for coaching, teaching, and mentoring five IP stations, and they visited each station almost every day. This time, however, they would be arriving in the middle of the night, unannounced.

The word on the street was that this particular IP station was serving as a base of operations for an illegal militia, the Jaysh al-Mahdi, that was engaging in sectarian violence, usually at night. As Pomfret and his Soldiers arrived at the station, they saw military-aged men fleeing in every direction.

"Don't chase them," Pomfret told his Soldiers. "I'll deal with this one."

Pomfret decided to hold the station commander accountable for the situation. Inside the station, however, the officer leadership was nowhere to be found.

Pomfret ordered his Soldiers to inventory the arms room. Almost half of the U.S.-provided weapons were missing. Pomfret surmised that the weapons were likely being used that night for extrajudicial killings of Sunnis and possibly for insurgent ambushes on his fellow Coalition Forces.

He decided to detain the highest-ranking authority present, the police station's Arms-Room NCO.

The next morning, Pomfret and his platoon headed back to the IP station. The platoon leader was determined to convince his counterpart that a commander is responsible for everything that happens under his watch.

Pomfret called ahead to the Iraqi Police station, as was his routine professional courtesy. Then, when his platoon was less than 100 meters from the station, an EFP rocked his lead vehicle.

It was the first time his platoon had been hit. One of Pomfret's NCOs was seriously wounded. The platoon's mission immediately shifted to casualty evacuation and vehicle recovery. The Iraqi Policemen at the station offered belatedly to assist, but the Americans took care of themselves, evacuating their wounded and recovering the destroyed vehicle.

The next day, Pomfret returned to the IP station, this time without calling ahead. He went directly into the commander's office.

The Iraqi Police major spoke first.

"I am very sorry to hear what happened to your soldier," he said, referring to the EFP blast. "I am also very sorry that you chose to detain one of my men," he continued. "I am sure this kind of thing never has to happen again. We can work together to kill the terrorists, and our men can be safe."

The Iraqi peered into Pomfret's eyes. The American platoon leader understood what was being offered: if Pomfret would agree to overlook the station's extrajudicial activities, then he and his Soldiers would be safe. If not, then they would be targeted.

My #1 mission is to bring all my Soldiers home alive, thought Pomfret.

The American officer stretched out his hand and shook on the unspoken agreement.

For the next four months in that AO, Pomfret worked with his IP counterpart to kill and capture Sunni insurgents—and his platoon faced no more ambushes.

56. JESSE ALLGEYER

Soon after the sniper round ricocheted harmlessly off the turret shield of one of his Humvee gun trucks, Lieutenant Jesse Allgeyer led a squad to search for the assailant. His platoon sergeant took a squad up to a roof to observe the area. Neither found any sign of the sniper.

Now Allgeyer was canvassing the neighborhood in search of information.

"Salaam Alaykum," he said to an elderly man sitting in a courtyard.

"Alaykum as-Salaam," the man replied.

"Thirty minutes ago, someone fired a weapon on this street," Allgeyer said through his interpreter. "Did you see anything, or do you know who might shoot at Coalition Forces?"

The man responded with feigned surprise.

"He says he didn't see or hear anything, and he doesn't know anything," reported Allgeyer's interpreter. "He says this neighborhood is safe."

"Sure, it's safe. That's what they always say," said a disgusted Allgeyer to his terp. "How can we provide security to people who won't cooperate with us?"

"They are scared," said the terp. "Many would help, but they fear being seen talking to the Americans. The militias or the al-Qaeda might punish them."

How could he get them to help without being seen? As Allgeyer pondered the question, he looked at his Humvee—and at the speakers that had recently been installed on it. The purpose of the speakers was crowd control, to warn Iraqi cars and crowds to move away.

A prior-service PSYOP specialist, Allgeyer had an idea. He scribbled a note:

"Help us make your neighborhood safe. Call 070072556 to provide information anonymously. We will act on your information."

"Charlie," Jesse said to his terp. "Translate this message. We're going to drive around the neighborhood with you announcing this over the loud speaker."

The number was to the company tip-line, a cell phone answered by the commander's terp.

Allgeyer's platoon drove slowly through the neighborhood over and over, announcing the tip line. He noticed several women cautiously entering the number into their cell phones as they heard the message.

After two hours, Allgeyer received a radio call from the company CP.

"Barbarian One-Six, this is Barbarian Six, over."

"This is One-Six," Allgeyer acknowledged.

"One-Six, I don't know what you're doing out there," said his commander, "but we've received 25 calls on the tip line in the last two hours. It looks like we already have what we need to roll up a sniper cell and a cache."

57. MIKE JOHNSTON

Lieutenant Mike Johnston reached across the Humvee and slapped his driver on the arm.

"It feels good to be in the middle of the pack for once," Johnston said.

Johnston was the platoon leader of his battalion commander's personal security detachment. Usually, Johnston's vehicle led their convoys.

Today, however, the battalion was occupying a new area of operations. American vehicles had not driven this road, Route Malibu, in months. They were moving into enemy territory, so a route-clearing element was in front of the PSD. Engineer vehicles led the movement, followed by a platoon of Infantry, then Johnston's element. Johnston's vehicle was just in front of his commander's, which was safely tenth in the order of march.

WHA-HOOOOOM!!!

The concussion shook Johnston's bones. For an instant he thought that he'd been hit, but then he realized that the explosion had occurred behind him—right where the battalion commander's truck would have been. Looking back, all he saw was a Humvee door sailing about 30 feet high through the air.

Johnston sent a quick contact report to battalion and then heard a radio report from his medic, who was in the truck behind the commander's.

"Polar Bear Six's truck is flipped upside down and off the side of the road!"

Johnston jumped out of his truck and started running back along the road. Debris was still falling. The first thing he noticed as he approached the vehicle was the massive crater—15 feet wide and 5 feet deep—that obliterated the raised roadway. Then he noticed blue Diet Pepsi cans strewn everywhere.

The blast had blown off the back hatch of the commander's Humvee, and the contents of its trunk had been jettisoned. Diesel fuel from the vehicle's cracked fuel tank was dripping over everything and everyone inside the upside-down truck.

The Humvee's nearside back door was open, and the first thing Johnston saw was the commander's interpreter, unconscious and suspended upside down by his seatbelt. The back third of his head was cracked wide open, his brain matter exposed. Johnson quickly looked forward into the TC's seat and assessed his commander, who was conscious and yelling in pain, bleeding from his ears and mouth.

Johnston attended first to the most serious injury. He began pulling the interpreter from the vehicle. The vehicle's driver joined him.

Johnston looked at the driver wearing only ACUs and instinctively felt a twinge of anger. *Where's your shit?* Then he saw the Soldier's IBA, still tangled on equipment in the upside-down driver's compartment. The driver had slipped out of his IBA in order to extricate himself from the vehicle and help others. Johnston felt proud to lead such men.

Together, Johnson and the driver pulled the interpreter out of the truck and up onto the road, where the platoon medic immediately began treating him.

Johnston and the driver turned their attention to rescuing their battalion commander. His door was combat locked, and the commander—dazed, bloodied, bruised, and soaked in diesel fuel—was having difficulty staying alert. Johnson worried that the vehicle would go up in flames at any moment. He coached his commander to unlock the door's combat lock. Johnston and the driver, both weight lifters, strained against the door, pulling with all their might to open it. But the door wouldn't budge.

Then Johnston remembered the "rat claw." When he had been at brigade headquarters a couple weeks earlier, the Brigade Safety Officer had handed him a prototype "rat claw" that had been developed to pull doors off Humvees. Only one per battalion had been issued. Johnston had thrown it into the trunk of one of his vehicles and hadn't given it another thought . . . until now. Fortunately, that vehicle was in the convoy today. Unfortunately, it was last in the order of march, at least 200 meters away.

Johnston sprinted down the road. He felt totally exposed. The IED had been command-detonated. He knew it was likely that he was being watched. His under-strength platoon had no dismounts to spare. His only protection as he ran along the raised roadway was his gunners atop Humvees, positioned 50 meters apart along his route.

Johnston arrived at the last vehicle. The back hatch wouldn't open.

Fuck!

He beat on it. No luck. He climbed up on the hatch and stomped up and down as hard as he could. Finally, the hatch popped. Johnson pulled the hatch open and dug through the gear to find the rat claw. It wasn't small. At one end was a large, heavy metal claw designed to clamp onto Humvee doors. Several long cables came off it, with hooks on their ends to affix to vehicles or winches. Johnston began his sprint back to the commander's destroyed truck. He held the claw on his chest with both arms, the cables resting over his shoulders, the hooks dragging along the ground behind him. Johnston, a collegiate athlete who prided himself on staying in top physical condition, was shocked at how exhausted he felt.

Arriving at his commander's Humvee, Johnston clamped the claw to the stuck door and then guided his own vehicle into position to hook up to the cables. It was time to attempt to pull the door off.

Everyone held his breath, hoping that a spark wouldn't set the vehicle on fire as the vehicle pulled forward. The door popped off without a hitch. The claw worked exactly as designed.

Johnston and the medic struggled to pull their commander out of the vehicle. He was a big man, and it seemed like every piece of equipment got stuck on everything possible as they attempted to extract him. As soon as they got him out and onto the ground, the commander went into shock. Doc, who had snaked a tube down the terp and was still treating him, gave verbal instructions to the driver, who successfully treated and stabilized his commander.

The interpreter died on the road. The platoon placed him into a body bag and laid it across the back seats of one of their trucks for the short trip to the patrol base. The gunner essentially had to sit on him, which he found upsetting. The terp was like a member of the platoon.

On what should have been a short movement, they found another IED alongside the road. Johnston and his platoon had to wait on the road for more than a half hour as an EOD team arrived and destroyed the ordnance in place. Johnston used the time to talk with his battalion TOC, correcting inaccuracies in earlier reports the TOC had received about the ambush.

MONTH EIGHT

58. KAI HAWKINS

"You fuck with my platoon, I'm gonna fuck you up," the outgoing platoon leader said.

Lieutenant Kai Hawkins couldn't tell if her predecessor was joking or serious. Still, it was an interesting welcome.

Hawkins was transitioning from the sprawling, urban-feeling FOB Striker to the Spartan outpost at Yusufiya, where she was now the only female officer on the patrol base. She was transitioning from a division-level platoon managing a massive supply warehouse to a truck platoon assigned to an Infantry battalion. This was Hawkins' fourth platoon, but her first that operated outside the wire.

It took only a short time for everyone in the AO to recognize Hawkins' reports on the radio, as hers was the only female voice on the net. She was cognizant that whenever she spoke, everyone knew it was her. She also sensed that her actions reflected on all women Soldiers, and she wanted to represent them well.

One day, her platoon was traveling along the dreaded Route Malibu, a narrow route where the elevated road enables insurgents to dig into the sides of the berm and embed IEDs under the roadway. Kai's platoon eased along the IED hot-spot, leery of the threat.

Everything seemed to be going fine.

BOOOM!

Adrenaline surged through Hawkins' blood. She jumped on the radio.

"Who's been hurt, who's been hit?" she said excitedly. "Somebody tell me something."

One of her NCOs quickly replied with a status report.

"Hey, this is Two-Eight. I've been hit, everything's fine, we're still rolling."

"Roger, let's get out of the kill zone," the new PL ordered. "Speed up and we'll assess the battle damage at the next checkpoint."

After a few moments, Hawkins' driver made a suggestion.

"Hey, ma'am, you need to call up battalion and give a report."

"Right."

Realizing the importance of projecting a calm voice over the radio, Kai took a deep breath before keying her mike.

"Polar Bear X-Ray, this is Fox Two-Six, over."

"This is Polar Bear X-Ray."

"Roger, we just hit an IED . . . ."

Hawkins sent a clear and succinct report to the TOC and continued her mission. She focused on projecting a calm voice, even though her heart was pounding.

After completing her report, Hawkins turned to her driver.

"So how many IEDs is this for you?" she asked.

"Oh, that makes 21."

Hawkins was shocked at how casually her driver had answered the question, as if 21 IEDs were no big deal.

59. DONNIE SUCHANE

Lieutenant Donnie Suchane led his platoon across a farm field under the cover of darkness. They were returning from an all-day dismounted patrol.

Six days earlier, one of Suchane's Soldiers had been killed by an IED as he moved along a path during daylight. Suchane had taken to heart the lessons of that day—move at night to defeat command-detonated IEDs; stay off trails to avoid pressure-plate IEDs.

Fa-RUMP!

Night turned to daylight for an instant as a fireball exploded on the platoon's flank. The platoon rushed to aid the Soldier who had been walking where the fireball erupted, but it was already too late. In a case of terrible luck, the Soldier had stepped on a pressure-plate IED in the middle of a farm field, one that had been emplaced by the enemy for an unrelated baited ambush. For the second time in a week, Suchane carried the body of one of his Soldiers to the MEDEVAC helicopter.

The bird drifted back into the night, leaving the platoon kneeling alone in the dark field.

Suchane returned to the platoon's perimeter. He saw shock and fright in his Soldiers' eyes. They had gone their first seven months without a casualty, and now in two of their last three patrols, they'd seen a friend killed—gruesomely and instantly, without warning.

They thought they were doing everything right, yet things were going terribly wrong. They waited silently in the field under the black sky.

"Sir, why don't we request an air extraction from here?" someone suggested to Suchane. "Who knows what else is buried between here and the patrol base?"

The platoon leader weighed the options.

One of his Soldiers broke the silence with a simple question.

"What do we do now, sir?"

Suchane knew his Soldiers were scared. He was, too. But he knew what he had to do.

"Guys, follow me," he said. "If anyone else is going to get killed tonight, it's going to be me."

The men formed a Ranger file behind their lieutenant, and he led them back to their company patrol base.

60. SHAWN JOKINEN

Route Coyotes was a problem for everyone, but its responsibility fell to Lieutenant Shawn Jokinen's platoon.

The route was considered a "Tier 1" IED site, one of the worst in Iraq.

Vehicles or not, Jokinen felt the best way to defeat the roadside bombs was to attack them with dismounted Soldiers—on foot.

So Jokinen sent his platoon aggressively patrolling the area, learning the terrain, investigating enemy patterns, proofing infil and exfil routes, identifying OP locations. After two weeks of development and planning, Jokinen's Soldiers were ready.

On mission night, the platoon's vehicles rolled into sector at 0300, weaving through the empty streets to a dismount point. Jokinen got on the ground and took five other men with him: a SAW gunner, a rifleman, a long-range marksman, a medic, and an interpreter. The vehicles drove back to the patrol base to stage as a quick reaction force.

Jokinen's tiny team slithered into position, clearing the area around an abandoned building before emplacing protective claymore mines outside and stepping inside the vacant structure.

In the darkness, Jokinen's team watched an area where they expected the enemy would attempt to emplace IEDs.

After about four hours, a sedan pulled to a stop near Jokinen's position. Four masked men leapt out of the idling car. A pair of them faced outward with AK-47s. The other two heaved three 155mm artillery rounds out of the back seat and began wiring them together. Jokinen was struck with the image of a NASCAR pit crew.

Then he gave the order to engage.

We're taking back Route Coyotes.

61. HERMAN BULLS

Lieutenant Herman Bulls felt an emptiness in the pit of his stomach that almost took his breath away. He was walking across his battalion area on the FOB, but his heart and mind were thousands of miles away.

He thought about his girlfriend whom he'd just talked to on the phone, about his grandfather who was living his final days, about the carefree life he'd once taken for granted. Bulls had never imagined that being a Soldier would demand such a high toll on his personal life.

How was it, he wondered, that he was sacrificing so much for his country when most Americans were sacrificing nothing? In his mind, it just wasn't right.

Opening the canvas flap that served as a door, Bulls entered the huge tent that housed his platoon. He paused and took in the scene: a Soldier watching a DVD on his laptop; a few others sleeping; four Soldiers seated around a folding table, playing cards, laughing. They all looked so young and carefree. It was incredible to think that twelve hours ago they had all been out on a mission—dirty, sweaty, tired, determined, lethal. These men never quit, never said no, never wavered in the face of the unimaginable horrors of combat.

A sense of gratitude and pride began to well up within Bulls. These great young Americans worked harder, longer, and in conditions more difficult than the folks at home could ever imagine. Every one of them had raised his right hand in a time of war and volunteered to personally pay the price so that millions of others could enjoy freedom. They were away from their families, too. Many of them were on their second or third deployment.

They were America's next "greatest generation"—whether or not the country would ever recognize it.

Bulls felt humbled to lead such people. He admired and loved them more than they would ever know. And for the next few months, at least, THEY were his family.

He approached the card game.

"Hey, L-T," a smiling Soldier said as he made space for another chair. "You're in the next hand."

62. TOM HICKEY

Lieutenant Tom Hickey and his mechanized Infantry platoon were maintaining part of an outer cordon for a clearing operation when he saw an Iraqi man running towards one of his Bradley Fighting Vehicles. The man held a child in his arms, his shirt and arms bright red with blood. His wife followed behind him.

The NCO in charge of the nearest Bradley jumped down to meet the man. Hickey did the same. When Hickey arrived at the scene, the NCO had already called for his BFV's ramp to be lowered.

"This little girl's shot in the neck," the NCO reported to Hickey. "We got to get her to Riva Ridge!"

"I'll go with you," said Hickey, who helped the family into the back of the Bradley and then sat there with them.

The three-year-old child had been struck by a stray AK-47 round that had skimmed her temple and lodged in her throat. She was bleeding from the head and neck and turning blue.

Hickey sent a SITREP to his platoon and ordered the other section of Bradleys to reposition to cover the gap in the cordon.

The Bradleys sped through the streets of Baghdad faster than Hickey had ever experienced. His platoon sergeant called ahead to the ECP at Camp Liberty, which permitted the pair of Bradleys to pass through at full speed.

When the Bradleys arrived at the medical clinic, they were met by a crowd of medical personnel who whisked the little girl inside as her parents followed behind.

Hickey looked at his watch. From the time he saw the girl until delivering her to the aid station, less than six minutes had passed. The child had a chance to live.

Walking back to the Bradley with the NCO, Hickey pondered aloud whether the platoon really should have reduced their combat power on a mission just to treat an unknown civilian child who had not been wounded by American weapons.

The NCO became choked up, tears welling in his eyes.

"Sir," said the father of three daughters to his bachelor LT, "when you have children, you'll understand."

63. JIM FREEZE

Jeff,

I've been thinking a bit about some of the things you wrote about. I definitely know where you're coming from on wanting to get over here and do your part. Before deploying, I had the same feelings that you did. I wanted to get over here and see what everything was like, see how I'd react under pressure.

About two weeks later, my whole perspective changed when we lost one of our own.

We were moving to secure a mortar firing site and my lead vehicle hit an IED directly under the driver's seat. Everyone started doing what we were trained to do. I was the second vehicle in the movement, so as the dust settled, we drove around to the front side of the disabled vehicle to see it on fire and one of my Soldiers lying halfway out of his driver's compartment, face down on the front of the Stryker. I immediately jumped out and got on top of the burning Stryker to try to pull him out. I just saw one of my Soldiers lying unconscious with flames around him and I did what I could to get him out.

I tried pulling him up from underneath his arms and as I did, I saw his uniform and t-shirt had already started to melt and the flesh on the small of his back was exposed and burnt. His face was also bloody and I think some of it was actually already melting to the armor.

As I frantically tried to tug him out, a flame jumped up and licked my face. Meanwhile, the gunner from that truck also tried to pull him out, but said he couldn't bear the heat anymore. Others were all around, spraying every fire extinguisher we had, but to no avail. Next thing I remember I was telling everyone on the ground to load back in the trucks. (We did all we could and we thought we were hearing shots, but they ended up just being rounds cooking off inside the vehicle.)

There was nothing more we could do besides watch the truck burn to the ground with one of our brothers still inside.

While we sat there, securing the site until another platoon could relieve us, I watched as one of my Soldiers' bodies burned. His head was still face down on the front of the slat, and I had to sit and watch his hair being singed away until his head was completely charred and flames completely engulfed him and the vehicle. I have a feeling that the image from that moment will be seared into my memory for as long as I live.

Four of us were evac'd to the Baghdad ER, mostly for precautionary reasons. After they treated me, I asked about my other guy and they took me to the trauma ward to see him.

When they showed him to me, I thought, "That's not him, he doesn't look like that." This guy's face was blackened and swollen and peppered with tiny pieces of Kevlar shrapnel and his eyes were swollen and crusted shut. It wasn't until I heard him say, "LT, is that you?" that I realized it really was in fact him. He hadn't heard yet, so the first thing he asked me was whether or not Crouch had made it out. I held his hand and we cried together for a little while.

My perspective about our role in the war changed drastically that day. No longer was I eager to go grab this war by the horns or volunteer to lead extra patrols. I think my men felt the same way.

For about a week after the attack, I had trouble sleeping, just replaying the events of the attack over and over in my head, wishing I did something different, something more. Even now, six months after the attack, there are times I sit awake at night for over an hour and wish I just kept trying to pull him out until I succeeded rather than giving up. I suppose I'll continue to feel this way for a long time.

God forbid anything like that should happen to you or to anyone else, but I share that story with you for a different perspective. I'm still very proud to serve in the Army. I'm very proud of my men and the good work we're doing over here. I can tell you first hand that we're seeing a real change over here. Iraqis are taking the lead on security and many other things.

A year plus is so long. The only thing keeping me going is the people around me going through the same suck.

I hope you're enjoying the States. If not for yourself, please enjoy it for me.

Jim

MONTH NINE

64. ISAAC WIDNASZ

Lieutenant Isaac Widnasz approached a man who was standing at a corner lot filled with cars parked closely together. Clearly the man was running an illegal parking business, which was one of the primary ways that the local militia funded its insurgency.

"What are you doing here?" Widnasz asked.

"I am selling apples," said the man.

The platoon leader looked around. He didn't see any apples.

"I don't see any apples," he said.

"I sold them all," replied the man with a shrug of his shoulders.

Peering into the bag full of cash the man was holding, Widnasz's latent anger exploded.

"You think I'm fucking stupid?!" he yelled, bumping into the shorter man. "You think I don't know you're JAM? I kill motherfuckers like you every night!"

The man stepped back and turned away. The LT followed behind him. He had more to say.

"Well, FUCK YOU and all the other piss-ants who lie like whores but won't do an honest day's work to build your country!"

Something caught Widnasz's attention. It was one of his squad leaders, who had moved around behind the man to make eye contact with his platoon leader. The NCO's face sent a clear message—"Calm down."

Widnasz immediately recognized that his NCO was right. He ceased his tirade. Turning away from the man, the PL signaled for the dismounted patrol to continue. He noticed that scores of Iraqis were looking at him, witnesses to the altercation.

Once the patrol had moved down the block, Widnasz stepped alongside the squad leader.

"I guess I pissed away all the 'good will' we gained by handing out school supplies this morning, eh?" he said, only half-kidding. "Thanks for straightening me out, Sergeant."

"No problem, sir," the NCO replied with a smile. "I know you'd do the same for me."

65. MATT MARTINEZ

Lieutenant Martinez's truck eased along at the head of the platoon, moving into a slender lane between two buildings. He usually positioned his truck second in the column, but had ended up in front after turning around in one of the narrow streets.

Matt sensed something was wrong; the area seemed barren and silent. The silence was shattered when the Humvee behind Matt's vaulted into the air with a fiery burst. The IED blasted straight into the cabin and spewed fuel throughout the compartment. PFC Nicholas Hartge was sitting in the rear seat when the explosion launched his body out the side of the vehicle, killing him instantly. The hood of the vehicle was on fire, and so was the gunner. The 250-pound gunner wasn't able to step onto the burning hood, so he jumped to the ground from the roof of the truck. The impact ripped compound fractures in both of his legs. Three other Soldiers exited the flaming Humvee, covered in burning fuel.

Matt jumped from his vehicle and saw the Humvee behind him ablaze with its doors open and Soldiers lying on the ground. One Soldier—on fire—ran toward him. Another Soldier walked aimlessly, his upper body partially on fire. The drivers of the two closest Humvees found their fire extinguishers and went to work. Matt had emphasized this so many times—the importance of the little things. *Know where the fire extinguisher is on every vehicle. Know how to use it. Pre-combat checks.*

Matt could hear the other half of his platoon engaged in a firefight with insurgents in an open area to his rear. The burning vehicle and Matt's truck were locked in a choke point. The immediate aid of the casualties depended on the few Soldiers with Martinez.

They rushed to the burning Humvee to pull the wounded men to safety. Ammunition inside the burning Humvee—.50 cal ammo, M203 grenades, M67 grenades—caught on fire and started cooking off. One of the Soldiers was hit in the side with shrapnel from the detonating ammunition while he was grabbing somebody near the truck. He fought through the intense heat to grab one of his wounded comrades, his own skin burning during the attempt. The other reacting Soldiers retrieved a backboard for one of the badly injured men and moved him to an alcove at a nearby house, where the medic tended to him.

I need to pull this platoon together, thought Martinez.

66. VICKI TAPPRA

Lieutenant Vicki Tappra and her platoon were returning from an all-day mission when they took a short halt on high ground along their route. It was 1900 hours, almost twilight.

As Tappra talked with her platoon sergeant, one of her gunners reported that a car was parked off to the side of the highway ahead of the platoon.

She decided to investigate.

119

As the platoon began to move toward the stopped vehicle, two Iraqi Police vehicles sped ahead, flashing their lights as they passed the car.

Tappra's platoon closed on the stopped vehicle.

Approaching the car with her interpreter, she saw a man behind the wheel.

"Why are you stopped here?" Tappra asked.

The man replied.

"He says his car is broken down," her interpreter said. "And the Iraqi Police have already stopped to help him. They are calling his family."

Tappra knew that that was a lie. The IP vehicles had sped past him.

One of Tappra's Soldiers reached into the vehicle and turned the key still in the ignition.

The engine started immediately.

"It doesn't seem to be broken down to me," she said.

The startled man had no explanation.

Another one of Tappra's Soldiers inspected the car's trunk, finding wire cutters.

The man fumbled for an explanation.

Then one of her squad leaders called out from down the road. He saw a lumpy garbage bag resting along the roadside about 50 meters away—*a possible IED.*

Tappra thought about what to do. Standard procedure was to secure the area and call for an EOD team to interrogate the suspected IED. That would take at least a couple of hours, and potentially much longer. Her Soldiers were already tired after a long day. Tomorrow would be another long day.

The bag either was or was not an IED, and there was only one person present who knew for sure—the liar now standing outside his car.

"Tell the man to go dump the contents of that bag," she told her interpreter. "If he does, we'll let him go. If not, we'll detain him."

The man walked towards the garbage bag. He seemed confident at first, but his pace slowed the closer he got.

About five meters away from the bag, the man stopped. Slowly he turned around and raised his arms in surrender, beginning to sob. Walking back to Tappra, he admitted that the garbage bag was an IED.

A swipe test indicated explosive residue on his hands.

Tappra then called EOD.

67. JASON KOSLOVSKY

Lieutenant Jason Koslovsky was sitting on his cot in his company's combat outpost when one of his Soldiers approached him, looking concerned.

"Sir, I'm worried about Jones," the Soldier told his PL. "He just gave me a care package he received. He never even *shares* anything from his packages."

Koslovsky thought about Jones. Jones had been upset and distracted ever since he'd returned from mid-tour leave. Things hadn't gone well with his wife. Jones suspected that she was cheating on him, and he wasn't at all happy with how she was taking care of their son.

"Thanks," Koslovsky replied. "I'll check up on him."

Koslovsky went straight to his platoon sergeant, who had been a drill sergeant for years.

"Sergeant," Koslovsky said to his right-hand man, "Jones is giving away things today. That's a sign of suicide, right?"

"Sure is, LT," replied the platoon sergeant. "I'll talk with him."

An hour later, Koslovsky's platoon sergeant reported back to him.

"It turns out that Jones just received a 'Dear John' letter from his wife, and on a phone call one of his friends told him that his wife is beating their son."

"Damn, that's rough," said Koslovsky.

"Jones had a plan to fucking end it all today," continued the NCO. "He was going to blow his own head off in the shitter. I talked with him and we've taken his weapon, but he needs Mental Health. We need to put him with an NCO escort onto the CLP this afternoon and get him back to the FOB."

"I'm glad you're my platoon sergeant," said Koslovsky, "and Jones should be, too."

68. BRAD MELLINGER

Lieutenant Brad Mellinger's platoon was given the task to recon and set up an ambush on a known al-Qaeda meeting location and training site. The building was set off by itself, with no other buildings within a kilometer of it.

Mellinger selected an old bombed-out bunker for his platoon's hide site, about two kilometers from the objective. They set up on the roof, set up their optics, and started observing the target building.

Throughout the morning, not much was going on. After a couple of hours of waiting, Mellinger and his men heard gunshots. They couldn't determine where the shots were coming from, or if they were directed toward his position. They finally saw a couple of enemy snipers kneeling near some brush, just shooting at random targets around the area.

"Don't engage," Mellinger said. "This may be a recon by fire, just to make sure the area is clear of Coalition Forces."

After a while, people from the target building drove their cars to the intersections leading into the area and set up blocking positions.

Soon, there was no more traffic passing the parked cars near the building except for those cars pulling into the meeting site. Brad observed six vehicles arrive at the meeting site.

Mellinger's men knew that something big was going down. Everything was coming into place to match their intelligence estimate: the enemy's operations, the security posture, even the meeting process. They believed it wasn't just a normal meeting, but a meeting for some higher-level guy who wanted to check in with the operational people in the area.

Mellinger wanted to allow as many enemy as possible to enter the area to inflict as many casualties as possible. There were now six vehicles at the building. However, he didn't want to wait too long to act and allow people to get away. A few vehicles left the site, and Mellinger's platoon noted the identifiable markings on them.

A few minutes later, the people at the target house lit up their fire pit and started cooking lunch. Mellinger started working support assets to initiate on the target building. He called Higher and requested an adjust-fire mission.

"Shot, over."

"Shot, out."

"Splash, over."

Mellinger heard the artillery incoming. The first round landed so far away that Mellinger wondered if it was the mission he'd called.

"Adjust fire, over."

There was no response.

Within a minute or two, a palm grove 800 meters away from the target building started erupting with multiple explosions.

This isn't an adjust-fire mission . . . they shot a fire-for-effect. And it's WAY off-target.

It appeared the people at the meeting were getting spooked by the artillery explosions, even though the rounds were so far off.

Mellinger expedited lining up air assets to conduct a strike on the building. He had to talk through his Higher to communicate with the A-10s that were searching for the target building.

"The aircraft can't see a building by itself. They see two buildings together," reported battalion.

Mellinger couldn't see that there was another building behind his target building.

"No, there's just one building by itself," he insisted.

Mellinger had sent a 10-digit grid to the target—and his estimate was off by a few hundred meters.

"The A-10s see a building at your grid, but it has no roof."

"I can't tell for sure, but it looks like it has a roof," Mellinger said.

The A-10s did a gun run on the building with no roof. Mellinger immediately knew that they were on the wrong target.

"Okay," Brad said. "Here's an adjustment to their target . . . ."

69. JARED OREN

Lieutenant Jared Oren and his platoon sergeant prepared to get to the bottom of an issue. The unit next to theirs on the FOB had been delayed five hours on a re-fueling mission earlier that day when a mission-critical component had disappeared from one of their trucks. That unit's leadership accused one of Oren's Soldiers of stealing the part and installing it on his own truck.

Oren's platoon sergeant called the Soldier's squad leader into the room.

"Sergeant, did you or did you not tell PFC Taylor to steal the part?" the platoon sergeant asked.

"Sergeant, I told him to 'go get the part and install it'," replied the squad leader. "I figured he'd go to Class Seven or Class Nine or whatever and pick it up."

The platoon sergeant shook his head.

He called the PFC into the room and asked him a similar question.

"Taylor, did you or did you not remove a part from an Alpha Company vehicle?"

The Soldier didn't say anything.

125

"PFC Taylor," said Oren. "It is in your best interest to come clean and say once and for all if you did it. We need an honest answer from you right now."

"Yeah", he admitted. "I mean, I saw they shit, and I took it, but it was my bad."

"Yes, it was your bad," said his platoon sergeant. "Get out of here and go back to work."

The squad leader remained in the room with his platoon leader and platoon sergeant.

"Sergeant," the platoon sergeant told him, "We hold you responsible for this. You can't give a Soldier a task and then walk away if you aren't sure he knows how to accomplish it. As the squad leader, it is your job to teach and to supervise your Soldiers. Any questions?"

"No, Sergeant," replied the squad leader.

"Sergeant," added Oren. "The best way to learn something is to teach it. And this incident indicates that at least some Soldiers in the platoon don't know everything they should. So, by this time next week, you need to be prepared to teach classes to the platoon on two subjects—how to get repair parts the right way, and the Army's ethical decision-making process."

70. BRYAN SMITH

It had been a day since Lieutenant Bryan Smith lost his RTO to an IED outside the chicken farm. Today, Smith's company commander tasked his platoon to go back to the chicken farm to repair the two IED craters and wait for the enemy to return.

Smith took a portion of his platoon back to the place where they'd lost the RTO, where several others had been wounded, where two Humvees had been destroyed. They cleared the route the same as the night before and then secured the area while the Engineers refilled the IED holes with concrete.

It wasn't terribly cold, but it was cool enough that the concrete needed extra time to dry, so Smith moved away from the site in order to overwatch the holes. He wanted to make sure no one put new bombs in the wet concrete, but he was hoping to catch anyone bold enough to try.

They watched the holes for eight hours. At 0400, Smith dismounted and personally put the sniper team into position to overwatch the holes. He then moved his mounted sections closer to a hide site where he could quickly reinforce the sniper team if necessary.

They waited, checking in with the sniper team every half-hour over the radio. The sniper team leader called at about 0715.

"Red One, this is Shadow. I've got four individuals with digging tools on the road digging in the concrete holes."

This was it. There's no doubt these guys are bad.

Smith notified his commander and gave his sniper the order to engage the diggers.

The snipers readied themselves to engage with their Barrett .50 caliber sniper rifle.

TOWWWW . . .

The deep thud of the Barrett bolted through the streets.

The snipers hit one of the diggers. The rest of diggers jumped into two "bongo" trucks and tore away from the chicken farm. They fled to the west, directly toward Smith's position.

Smith started his patrol moving east on Route Hurricanes, toward the chicken farm and toward the fleeing insurgents. Smith saw the bongo trucks driving right at them. They were 300 meters away. The diggers saw Smith's vehicles and yanked the bongo trucks off course. One truck cut to the north, down another road. The other truck U-turned and went back the other way.

"Sergeant, you follow the truck that turned around on Route Hurricanes, I'll take my section to the north after the other truck."

"Roger."

Smith's section sped after the first truck, but they couldn't close the gap. The bongo truck screeched to a stop at a canal. The insurgents jumped out and disappeared into the canal, lost in the reeds.

Smith's section dismounted and started clearing both sides of the canal. They didn't see anything. He called for air support. A couple of his Soldiers started searching the bongo truck: explosives, weapons, video recorder.

The AH-64 Apaches came on station.

"Roger, can you give me a fly-over?" Smith asked. "Just buzz the canal, get me some rotor wash on those reeds."

No insurgents.

"Alright, go ahead and engage with your gun."

The Apaches ripped off some rounds from the 30mm cannons. Smith's guys again searched through the reeds. Nothing.

I should've engaged these guys when I had a chance, back when we first saw them.

The other section had better results. They had chased down the other bongo truck, pulled out the insurgents, put them on the ground, and bound them with zip-ties. A search of their bongo truck yielded a pressure-plate "speed bump" IED, digging tools, AK-47s, and ammunition. The detainees had multiple forms of identification on them. The section sergeant loaded the insurgents into his Humvees and hauled them back to the patrol base.

Smith's section pulled into the patrol base and linked up with the rest of the platoon. That's when he saw the captured insurgents.

These are the guys that killed my RTO. They laid the IED. They took him from us, from his family. He was my RTO, the guy I talked to every day, the guy I messed around with, one of my friends.

He's one of my Soldiers, one of the guys I care about—that I love.

Anger and pain raged deep inside Smith, the most intense hatred he'd ever felt.

He pulled himself back, restrained himself. He had to make sure his own guys were okay.

He knew that lashing out at the detainees based on his emotions would make his Soldiers' time there longer and likely harder for the next unit coming into this AO.

Smith then worried about how his Soldiers were going to react to the detainees. Bryan's was a platoon of Infantry guys.

These guys won't think twice about kicking a guy's ass.

Smith turned to check in on his Soldiers. The men were obviously hurting, but they were professional. They had been trained well. They had good leaders. And they were strong enough to do the right thing.

They didn't do anything stupid that could've gotten the detainees released—something like sending the detainees to court beaten, with black eyes. The best they could do was trust that the system would work.

Hopefully, these guys are gonna go away to prison for the rest of their lives.

Smith gathered himself and made sure the platoon was okay. Then he sat down to write a letter of condolence to his RTO's mom.

71. JOHN NGUYEN

Lieutenant John Nguyen reviewed the weekly patrol schedule that he'd just received from his battery commander. Looking at it, he concluded that there wasn't sufficient "re-gen" time between missions for his Soldiers. For several consecutive days, his platoon's missions had extended much longer than planned. In addition to regular patrolling, they had been working with SIGINT assets to raid targets and seize detainees, and processing the detainees sometimes lasted until the start of the next mission.

The problem was that when time on missions increased, the time needed for vehicle 10-level maintenance and sleep didn't decrease. As a result, what got squeezed out was "re-gen" time, as Nguyen liked to call it—time to call home, play some X-Box, work out, listen to music. Personal time to unwind. Nguyen had come to view the deployment as a marathon, not a sprint. His Soldiers had no weekends or days off—just day after day of relentless missions. Nguyen had noticed that his Soldiers weren't as alert mentally outside the wire when *all* they'd done recently was work and sleep. They needed their re-gen time.

Nguyen approached his battery commander.

"Sir," he said. "With the new mission set, our OPTEMPO has increased significantly, and the guys are smoked. They've had no opportunity over the past week to call home, get on email, go to the gym, anything like that."

John pulled out a troop-to-task matrix that he and the other PLs had developed along with their PSGs.

"Sir," he continued. "Mission, maintenance, minimal sleep—we're getting those accomplished, but there's been no time for personal 're-gen.' Look at how tight it's been," he said, pointing at the troop-to-task matrix.

"What do you have in mind?" asked his commander.

"Sir, if we can cut an hour off the front and back ends of these patrols," he said, pointing at the chart, "and cut Second Section's patrol on Monday, everyone should have time to re-charge their batteries. We can still get all the missions accomplished. We'll just have a little less time in sector. And this assumes we don't get any more patrols-from-hell in the next few days."

"That sounds reasonable, John," replied his BC. "Your changes won't impact any other platoons, so you can run with them. Why don't you update the patrol board in Ops and I'll put it out to the other platoon's tomorrow."

"Hooah, sir. Thanks."

MONTH TEN

72. TRAVIS ATWOOD

Lieutenant Travis Atwood sat in his room on the COP. He rubbed his temples. Exhausted. The room faded for a moment.

He woke up a few seconds later. His muscles ached. Nonstop, patrol after patrol, he was nearly spent from pulling double duty—both as platoon leader and platoon sergeant. He was patrol leader for every mission outside the COP, with no rest cycle between his two jobs. Meanwhile, his platoon sergeant stayed on the FOB, a shadow of the Soldier Atwood knew him to be. His PSG won't ride in anything lighter than a Bradley. It's not so much *fear*, but a sound logic driven into his mind by his gunner's death and his own wounding by the same grenade. "If we have Bradleys, we should use them," he says.

But the terrain gets a vote too, and BFVs can't fit down the AO's narrow streets and alleyways. A change to Bradleys would severely reduce the platoon's maneuverability in battle.

Atwood closed his eyes and imagined various scenarios: IEDs, ambushes, complex ambushes, cordon and searches. He envisioned them with and without Bradleys. In some situations, the added armor would help. In others, insurgents would escape down alleys or the vehicles would get stuck in a bad situation. But when he imagined a battle without his platoon sergeant, Atwood just felt more exhausted.

Atwood thought about the best interests of the platoon. On one hand: no armor, but no platoon sergeant. On the other: more personnel, and a senior NCO to help manage the chaos and tend to casualties.

He came to believe that sometimes compromise is necessary. He could live with two BFVs, two Humvees, and a respected and competent platoon sergeant.

So he gave in to his platoon sergeant's request. Atwood rubbed his eyes again. He'd need to start brainstorming new TTPs before he could go to bed.

73. MIKE HESS

Lieutenant Mike Hess lay prone on the cool ground, motionless, covered by leaves, observing a farmhouse and field through his binoculars.

The evening before, his squadron had cleared through the area. They had received intelligence that significant caches were buried at the farm, but their efforts to find a cache had been fruitless. Time and again, Hess's Soldiers had identified potential caches in the field by using metal detectors, only to find that the signal was merely scrap metal that had been buried there to frustrate the American technology. At one point, Hess had looked around at the Iraqis observing the scene from a distance, wondering who among them were laughing as his Soldiers labored in the heat chasing false leads. The insurgents may as well have painted "the finger" on each chunk of metal.

As darkness had fallen last night, the squadron had abandoned its efforts and prepared to move to its next objective.

Hess's squadron commander and company commander had approached him.

"Mike," his SCO had said. "The bad guys know we use metal detectors, and they fooled us today. But they're predictable, too. I'll bet they return to do their own BDA after we leave. So, I want your platoon to do a stay-behind OP tonight. We'll let them lead us straight to their caches."

Under the cover of darkness and amid the movement out of the area of two companies of Soldiers, Mike's platoon and the squadron's sniper platoon had settled into their hidden observation posts.

Darkness gave way to dawn, and Iraqis began emerging from their homes.

"Charlie One-Six, this is Two, over," whispered a squad leader over his radio.

"One-Six," Hess replied.

"We got two men, unarmed, who approached from the east and are looking around the field."

"Roger," Hess said. He immediately called the report to Higher, which put ISR assets on station.

Hess's Soldiers observed as the two men investigated several specific locations, even digging up one cache to be sure it was there. A UAV recorded it all.

As the men left the farm field, Hess gave the order to capture them, and his Soldiers did so without incident.

Later that morning, the squadron returned to the farm. This time, they knew exactly where to dig. They found and exploited an extensive system of high-value caches. Both men turned out to be AQI operatives, and their information led rapidly to several more successful operations against AQI.

Who's laughing now? thought Hess. *Chalk one up for the good guys.*

74. MATT ROWE

Lieutenant Matt Rowe knew that he had two important decisions to make—which route to take back to the FOB, and whether to drive "white light" or "blackout." These were not unusual decisions;

he made them almost every mission. Yet tonight, for some reason, they felt unusually significant.

Rowe was in downtown Baghdad with half of his platoon at approximately 0200 hours on a warm May night. The EOD team that he was securing had just cleared a site. It was time to return to the FOB.

Now Rowe had to select the route. All routes from his location were categorized as "black"—to be used only when absolutely necessary due to the high frequency of IEDs. No route appeared any better than the others. That night, he noticed an unusually high number of military-age males milling around on the streets, watching the American Soldiers. Rowe decided to take the same route home. It was the most direct route, and an hour before it had been safe, which was more than he knew about other possible routes. To mitigate the risk, Rowe directed his patrol to drive on the left side of the roadway, which was different than how they had approached the area.

Rowe also decided to have his platoon move with their vehicle headlights on. It was a trade-off. Headlights enable Soldiers to more readily identify pressure-plates and roadside IEDs, but they also make it easier for an insurgent triggerman to accurately target a vehicle with a command-detonated IED. Rowe picked his poison. Based on his knowledge of the threat in the area, he judged the main threat to be infrared-activated EFPs, which are best countered by visual ID. He decided to keep the headlights on.

Convoying back, Rowe's truck was second on the order of march.

WHHHHOOOOOMMM!!!

A flash to his front.

"White 3 is hit! White 3 is hit!" screamed the lead vehicle's driver over the net. White 3 was SSG Martinez, the TC of the lead truck and senior NCO on the mission.

"How bad?" Rowe asked.

"He's unconscious."

"Is your vehicle still operational?"

"Yes."

Rowe knew that a small American FOB nearby had an aid station manned by a PA. Given the severity of the injury, he decided to continue toward the extensive medical facilities at the International Zone.

"Keep moving, straight to the IZ," Rowe ordered.

Whomp-WHHHHOOOOOMMM!!!

Two near-simultaneous blasts lit the sky in front of Rowe—one about 20 meters to his front, the other about 100 meters out. He heard small-arms fire, and then the louder return fire of his vehicles' gunners.

Rowe's mouth went dry and he got a sinking feeling in his stomach. He tried to look through the small windows in his up-armored HMMWV with his NVGs, but he could see only the green silhouettes of darkened buildings. His platoon was stopped in one of the few places in Baghdad with streetlights. He felt like they were actors on a stage, seen by all yet unable to see into the darkness beyond the spotlights.

With his gunners pouring 7.62mm into the darkness, the attackers withdrew. The shooting stopped, replaced by the low rumble of the idling vehicles. After taking a quick drink of water to regain his voice, Rowe called for reports and moved his truck forward to pull security for the now-heavily damaged lead truck. The two trucks behind him were unharmed.

As his platoon's mission transitioned to treating the casualties, Rowe wasn't sure what he should do.

Get out and evaluate? Stay on the radio and report? Become a casualty myself? The section leader is already down . . .

Rowe's driver hurried to render first aid. Two of the EOD personnel rushed forward. They carried the injured gunner into their EOD vehicle and began treating him. The driver was less seriously wounded. Rowe's antenna was damaged, so he typed out reports and a request for the QRF using his Blue Force Tracker.

Rowe's driver ran back and reported to his lieutenant.

"Sergeant Martinez is dead," he said.

"Are you sure?" asked Rowe.

Rowe's gunner interjected in disbelief.

"He's not dead. He's probably just unconscious," said the gunner.

It seemed impossible to believe that this strong and respected leader, Rowe's friend and sidekick on more than 160 missions, could be dead.

Rowe's driver ran back to the first truck, checked again, and returned.

"He's dead, sir. I know a dead body when I see one."

The QRF arrived. Rowe had his rear truck come forward and hook a tow strap to the immobilized vehicle, and they towed it back to the nearby small FOB.

As soon as the platoon entered the gate, they were swarmed by Soldiers. People pulled the casualties from the vehicles. They began asking for battle-roster numbers, casualty feeder cards, debriefings. Rowe wanted first to call his commander and tell him personally what had happened, since all he had been able to do with the BFT was type messages.

Then it hit him. *All of this is crazy. My number-one priority needs to be checking on my guys who are injured.*

Rowe walked away from the crowd and into the aid station. He first saw SPC Jinks. Jinks was laying on a gurney, in terrible pain from shrapnel wounds to his groin area. The medics were cutting the clothes off his body. Rowe took the hand of the 21-year-old father of three and held it.

Then Rowe saw Sergeant Martinez's body lying alone on a gurney nearby. A wave of grief consumed him. He felt like he couldn't breathe. He broke down momentarily, his tears flowing for his fallen brother in arms. Rowe watched as medical personnel respectfully placed Sergeant Martinez into a body bag.

Rowe went to the FOB CP and called his commander on the phone, explaining to him what had happened. After Rowe hung up, the FOB commander took Rowe aside and offered words of consolation. Then the FOB S-3 and S-2 began their de-briefing of the platoon leader. Rowe recounted his unit's mission and actions.

At one point, when Rowe was explaining his thought processes for selecting the route, the S-3 misunderstood him and emotionally interjected, "That's the worst route you could have taken! That's terrible!" As calmly as he could, Rowe explained that he had only considered the "terrible" route, but had decided on a route that was essentially the same one that the major recommended. This time the S-3 expressed approval. But the damage was done. Rowe felt defensive, like he was on trial.

Satisfied, the majors dismissed Rowe. Rowe trembled inside, furious that field grades who'd probably never led a combat patrol were scrutinizing his decisions. Rowe didn't need anyone to second-guess his decisions that night; he was taking care of that on his own.

Rowe gathered all his Soldiers together outside. They were in shock, chain-smoking even worse than usual.

He told them that they could say whatever they wanted, and they did. Their words seethed with anger at Iraqis. The IEDs had been command detonated, and there had been so many Iraqi men observing them from the moment they had entered the neighborhood.

Rowe's gunner reached up onto their truck's turret and grabbed a miniature Iraqi flag that had gotten snagged on it earlier that evening.

He held it out and lit it on fire.

As two of his Soldiers privately watched the flag burn with satisfaction, Rowe kept his counsel. He knew he shouldn't condone the activity, but it wasn't time for a philosophical civics lesson. His Soldiers needed to grieve, and burning the Iraqi flag wasn't going to hurt anybody.

Rowe was informed that a helicopter was inbound to collect SSG Martinez's remains. He had argued earlier with the captain who served as FOB mayor that he wanted to carry SSG Martinez's body back to their FOB with the platoon convoy, the body bag laid across the back seat of his Humvee. Rowe wanted to stay by his squad leader's side as long as he could and take him home. But he had been overruled. So, before the helicopter arrived, Rowe took his Soldiers into the aid station to pay their final respects. The body bag was still on the gurney, now covered with an American flag. The Soldiers gathered around their fallen leader, in silence and then in prayer.

After the helicopter departed with SSG Martinez's body, Rowe led a convoy back to their FOB. They moved out at dawn along the same street where they had been attacked four hours earlier. With Rowe's three operational trucks, two EOD trucks, two wreckers—one carrying the destroyed vehicle—and three other trucks, the convoy had the look and feel of a caisson in a funeral procession.

Iraqi people on the street stopped to watch them go by, and it seemed to Rowe that they understood what he was feeling. It occurred to him how many Iraqis had been killed in the war—how many of their own funeral processions these people had seen—and he felt sympathy for them. For the first time since the attack, Rowe's anger began to lessen.

Back at his FOB, Rowe was busy all morning reporting on what had happened. He talked with the task-force commander and the other field-grade officers, filled out storyboards that were sent to Higher, reviewed the battalion's duty log to fill in the blanks and correct its mistakes. Just before noon, his battery commander told him that he could join a convoy to visit the injured Soldiers, who were in the IZ. Rowe grabbed toiletries and clothes for both his wounded Soldiers and grabbed a photo album at the request of SPC Jinks. They rolled out at approximately 1200 to spend the afternoon at the CSH.

As he entered the hospital, Rowe passed by a lieutenant he remembered as a classmate from West Point. Looking back, he watched the lieutenant approach a group of Soldiers gathered in front of the hospital. It was obvious that they had just lost one of their brothers. Rowe visited with Jinks and was able to pick up the driver injured in the blast, who was RTD. They returned to their FOB in time to eat some chow. It had been more than 24 hours since Rowe had last slept or eaten.

Rowe wanted to attend the ramp ceremony at the airport, where he and others could pay respects as SSG Martinez's body was loaded on a plane bound for the United States.

He was told that the ceremony could go at any time after 1800, so Rowe stayed awake, waiting. As the hours lingered on, he decided to call his parents. As he told them what had happened, they became very upset. For the first time in his life, Matt heard his father cry. Hearing his usually stoic father worried literally to tears, Rowe felt sick with guilt, like someone had reached into his gut and was twisting his innards.

"I'll be alright," Rowe assured his parents. But they all knew it was a promise he couldn't guarantee.

Rowe drifted to sleep at about 0100, his first sleep in more than 40 hours.

An hour later, he was awoken by the alert for the ramp ceremony. A convoy of 16 trucks, led by Rowe's battalion commander and CSM, rushed to the airfield in the middle of the night.

Waiting at the flight line for the aircraft to arrive, Rowe saw another lieutenant there for the same reason. Rowe recognized him from a mission a week earlier in Amariyah. The other LT told Rowe that his Soldier had been killed by a sniper. Rowe recalled that during the mission in Amariyah, a sniper round had barely missed him. *It could just as easily be me here in the casket.*

It occurred to Rowe that, in the past 14 hours, he had run into two fellow lieutenants who were going through the same awful experience that he was. *This isn't some unique tragedy of mine. It's what happens every day in war, and leaders have to deal with it and continue to do their best.*

The C-130 arrived. The Hercules spit out a load of Soldiers returning from mid-tour leave, and then the plane's crew readied it to carry home Soldiers who would never again visit with their families.

Rowe had selected himself and the Soldiers of SSG Martinez's squad—those who had been on the fateful mission—to carry his casket onto the aircraft. An E-5 from a unit at the airfield gave them directions on how to carry the casket and what to do. Three caskets were being loaded that night. One did not have any Soldiers from its unit there for the ramp ceremony, so Rowe volunteered his detail to carry that casket as well.

Soldiers from both units lined up on the flight line, silently saluting.

First, the other platoon leader and his Soldiers carried their fallen comrade onto the aircraft. Then, the E-5 returned to march Rowe's team as they carried SSG Martinez. The E-5 did not keep a good cadence, and the pall bearers got out of step, which angered Rowe.

Rowe was struck by how cold and wet from condensation the casket handle was on his hands.

This casket must be packed with ice.

After placing SSG Martinez's casket where the E-5 directed, beside the first casket, Rowe and his Soldiers returned for the third casket. When they returned to the aircraft with the third body, there was no room to place the third casket. They were stuck holding the casket above the other two. There was no space for the pall bearers to move. Rowe's anger built.

Does this idiot have no fucking idea how important it is to do this right! We're trying to honor these Soldiers, and we're jacking it up!

Rowe took charge of the situation.

"Right step, march!"

After placing the casket down in an open space, they saluted. Then everyone present marched up around the bay of the aircraft, and a chaplain said a few words.

Immediately after the ceremony, Rowe raced back across the FOB, changing his radio's cryptographic fill along the way. He and 3rd Squad had to be ready to assume the EOD-security mission at 0600.

They were driving straight to the DFAC to get some breakfast when they received a mission before they could even get there. Less than 15 minutes later, Matt Rowe and 3rd Squad, with its new squad leader, rolled out the gate into Baghdad.

75. TED KRESBOK

Lieutenant Ted Kresbok was leading a route-clearance mission in the middle of the night along a rural highway. His platoon approached an Iraqi Army checkpoint.

"There are no IA present," reported the lead truck. "The checkpoint is abandoned."

It was the same old shit. Time and again in his route-clearing experiences, Kresbok had noticed that when the IA were absent, an IED was present. Kresbok's Soldiers increased their vigilance.

"I've got an EFP off the right side of the road," reported the lead truck. It was less than 100 meters from the IA checkpoint.

"This is bullshit," Kresbok commented to his crew. "The IA know where the IEDs are, but they leave us to get killed."

Kresbok's platoon had lost one of their own to an EFP. With every incident like this, he and his Soldiers became angrier with the Iraqis for their complicity.

After reducing the EFP, Kresbok's platoon began to move forward again.

As Kresbok's Humvee approached the checkpoint, the Iraqi flag flying there caught his attention.

"Stop here for a second," Kresbok told his driver. The lieutenant hopped out of his truck and snatched the Iraqi flag. "We're the ones risking our lives to give their country a chance. This flag is more ours than theirs."

Five minutes later, Kresbok radioed the local U.S. Army unit to send a report.

"Ironclaw Three-Six," interrupted the battalion's XO, a major. "Do you know anything about an Iraqi flag being taken from a checkpoint?"

Kresbok didn't take the question seriously. His impulsive action of taking the flag wasn't a big deal, and he didn't think it merited such a serious tone.

"Why, no, sir," he replied. "I don't know anything about an Iraqi flag."

Ten minutes later, the battalion XO called back.

"Ironclaw Three-Six, we are receiving reliable reports from our partner Iraqi Army unit that an American route-clearance patrol stole their national flag from one of their checkpoints. You are the only American unit in the area. YOU NEED TO FIND THAT FLAG!"

"Roger, sir," Kresbok admitted. "I have the flag and will return it immediately."

"Three-Six, who are you? What is your name?" asked the field-grade officer.

"Lieutenant Ted Kresbok, sir," he replied. He felt sick by his emerging realization of what he had done.

Kresbok swung his patrol around and returned the Iraqi flag to the checkpoint, which was once again manned by the IA.

When the patrol was complete, Kresbok was told to wait outside his battalion commander's office. He stood there throughout the night until well past daybreak. That morning, he was called in to face his battalion commander.

The day before, LT Ted Kresbok had been the battalion's "golden boy" platoon leader. Now he was a thief, a liar, an embarrassment to his unit.

76. TOM HICKEY

Lieutenant Tom Hickey sat in his up-armored Humvee, watching as one of his Bradley Fighting Vehicles burned to the ground 200 meters down the street. This time, thank God, all of his Soldiers had safely evacuated the vehicle after it was struck by an IED and caught fire. There was nothing to do now but watch it burn.

It appeared that everyone in the neighborhood had the same idea. Crowds surrounded the conflagration, apparently unfamiliar with the concept of rounds cooking off.

Hickey noticed a man approaching the burning Bradley. He threw something on it. Trash! Others imitated his example, and in short time a crowd of young men were heaping trash onto the vehicle, feeding the flames to the cheers of the crowd.

"Should I fucking light them up?" asked his gunner, who was manning the M240 machinegun.

ROE checklists filtered through Hickey's mind. *Destroying US government property.* That was enough to justify killing the bastards adding fuel to the fire.

He knew an investigation would clear him if he did open fire. And he knew it would feel good to kill some of the scumbags who were dancing around the Bradley like it was some kind of celebration. He wouldn't lose any sleep over killing them. But then he thought about something that had happened a few months ago.

"You remember that little girl who had been shot by a stray round in the neck, the one we rushed to the clinic?" he asked his crew.

"Yes, sir," the gunner replied.

"Well, we were saying then that people who can't control their fires and who harm innocent people should burn in hell, right?"

"Yes, sir."

"Well, there's no way we could engage the scumbags without some rounds hitting innocent people in the crowd."

His crew thought about it.

"Roger. Can I fire some warning rounds to scare them off?" the gunner asked.

"Roger. One burst center mass into the Brad."

That was enough to scare off the revelers.

77. TREVOR BUCKEY

"I'm sorry, but you're not going to Mental Health."

Lieutenant Trevor Buckey knows he is taking a huge risk in denying the request. But what is he to do? He had deployed a full mechanized Infantry platoon to combat, but now the platoon barely had enough men to operate. Casualties, R&R, taskings, now mental health.

Buckey knows what PTSD looks like. He's talked to his PA about the legitimate signs. He's sent other Soldiers away before, but now he just can't afford to. The mission would be at risk.

He's given advice for dealing with stress: "Take a baseball bat to that burnt-out car. Spend some time on the PlayStation. Get a little rack." But he can't afford to lose another body.

These days, when Buckey gets on the ground to clear a house or search some cars, he feels more like a squad leader, with only eight other Soldiers.

Buckey had gone on every patrol for the first five months of the deployment before burning himself out. And so he chose to back off a little, stay on the FOB for some of the missions.

Yeah, I should be with my Soldiers, but if there is a patrol I can't stay awake on, I'm not doing any good. I'm on my sixth straight month of having four hours of sleep a night . . . .

The Soldier who claims PTSD doesn't get a choice. His platoon needs him, and so his PL makes a decision: *you don't need mental health. You can take an hour on the PlayStation, or read or sleep or work out. But I need you at SP time.*

The irony of allowing someone time off is that it compounds the problem. If you give a guy some time away to decompress, then everyone else works that much harder to cover for him, making them that much more fatigued, that much more in need of time off.

The cycle drives the health meter downward until the game is in jeopardy—not enough energy pellets on the screen to go around.

Not going well?

Rebooting is not an option.

78. BRENDAN GRISWOLD

Lieutenant Brendan Griswold knew that many of his Soldiers felt helpless, angry, even scared by what had occurred. None of them said it explicitly or displayed it by their actions, but he knew what they were feeling, and he expected that he and his platoon sergeant would have to talk to them about what happened. But there was no time for that now. Security came first, and the combat outpost needed to be fully established.

For the next 48 hours, Griswold's Soldiers pulled long hours on security as follow-on Logistics and Engineer units worked to fortify the new COP. Enemy attacks continued—small arms and mortar attacks—and Griswold's Soldiers responded bravely and professionally. When his platoon was finally relieved from perimeter security, Griswold brought his Soldiers together to talk about what they had experienced. Last week, they had been first on the scene when six of their brothers in 1st Platoon were killed.

Griswold began by giving the platoon a SITREP on the AO. Then he asked his Soldiers to speak up if they had anything to say about what happened to 1st Platoon. No one responded. The platoon sergeant spoke.

"It's okay to feel worried," the platoon sergeant said. "And if anyone needs to talk to the chaplain, just let me know."

After a few moments of silence, one of the Griswold's Soldiers spoke up. He was a close friend to several of those killed in the attack.

"Let's go kill bad guys," he said solemnly.

Griswold knew what he meant. They had to put their grief behind them and focus on accomplishing the mission their comrades had died for.

The platoon bowed in prayer for a moment and then got back to work.

79. CLINT SPEEGLE

Lieutenant Clint Speegle woke up again, with the same face burned into his mind. He thought again about the first time he had seen that face.

It had been a routine day on a combat air patrol. A couple of troops-in-contact, a couple of route-clearance support missions, and

Speegle was nearing the end of the day. Then he got a call about a possible sectarian violence incident.

"Sunnis are firing belt-fed tracer rounds into a Shia neighborhood and lighting the houses on fire."

The unit had recently changed its TTP to fly at 6,000 feet to avoid small arms and RPG fire from the ground. Speegle thought at 6,000 feet they'd never be able to find the Sunni machine gunners, especially since the damage had already been done to the houses.

Whatever. This is stupid. We are never gonna find these guys. It happened 30 minutes ago, the houses are already burning. These guys are long gone.

Speegle's wingman continued to scan the area near the burning houses. He spotted a group of men loading machine guns into an SUV, 300 meters across the canal from the burning houses.

Speegle couldn't believe it. This was too easy. He was ready to shoot. However, he had to wait for clearance of fires over the radio. While they were waiting, the SUV drove away. Speegle and his wingman followed the truck as it drove to a house. Speegle saw kids playing in the yard.

Please drive away from that house.

The SUV drove away from the house and stopped at a mosque. Due to ROE, the Apache pilots couldn't shoot near the mosque. An individual exited the mosque and got in the SUV. The SUV departed the mosque and started driving down a canal road. Speegle's wingman nosed it over, and Speegle started shooting the vehicle with 30 mm cannon. The insurgents had no idea the Apaches were there until the ground started exploding around them. The lead aircraft broke off and Speegle made a run to engage the vehicle. One of the individuals started running from the vehicle.

"Oh no, dude, don't run," Speegle said. At one point, the fleeing individual laid down.

"Cease fire," Speegle said.

The individual got back up and started to run again.

"Alright, Brian, push it over. We need to get this guy."

Speegle started shooting alongside the fleeing individual, who was zig-zagging in between bursts of machine gun fire. He jumped into a ditch and kept fleeing.

The Apache had swooped down from 6,000 feet. Speegle was heads-down during the descent, tracking and engaging the enemy. When Speegle finally looked up, he was looking into the startled face of the insurgent, as the Apache hovered 75 meters away from him. Speegle pulled the trigger, turning the insurgent's body into a puff of pink mist.

But that face was still there, and Speegle knew he'd likely see it again the next time he slept.

MONTH ELEVEN

80. DAVE MACPHAIL

Make contact with the smallest element possible.

That was Dave MacPhail's mentality when he decided to listen to his NCOs. And so he put one man on point to lead a *vehicular* patrol.

His smallest element: one man in a dune-buggy-looking vehicle called a Husky. It was a mine-detecting vehicle with no weapon system.

MacPhail knew that innovation could be risky. *Nothing ventured, nothing gained.*

His new TTP was soon tested. A 5-array, passive-infrared-activated EFP exploded towards the point vehicle. It was an ambush that would've taken out the entire crew of a Humvee or RG-31, as it had on Christmas Day.

Dave's Soldiers reacted to the blast, swarming the Husky with security and searching for enemy to engage. They pulled the Husky driver out.

The extent of his wounds: merely a bad concussion. The new TTP worked.

81. JAMES ANDERSON

Lieutenant James Anderson's platoon had been doing a "speed day" up and down Route Tampa, which meant they would sit in one spot for about 15 minutes, then move on to another position. They had just passed through Checkpoint 101, north of Taji. This area was a hot spot, an area known for enemy activity.

As Anderson's tank pulled through the checkpoint, he noticed a woman getting out of a car. Normally, he wouldn't think anything about it. But in this area, he was alert to every movement around him. Anderson was concerned for her safety.

Nearing the woman, he noticed something unusual. *Man, that is a tall woman. Women in Iraq are rarely over six-feet tall and not as skinny as this woman.* But as they pulled forward, he didn't think much more about it.

Then something else struck Anderson as odd: the woman was wearing gloves. *Strange.* It must have been at least 80 degrees that day. He assessed the situation. *We have a tall, thin woman, wearing gloves, in a hot spot.*

As Anderson's tank eased closer to the woman, she covered her face a bit more. Anderson became even more troubled.

I could look at her hands. The difference between a man's hands and a woman's is pretty significant. If that doesn't work, I can ask her to move her veil.

He pulled his tank up next to the woman and popped the hatch. He stuck his head out the hatch and motioned to get the woman's attention. He told her to put her hands up. He took off his own gloves to demonstrate.

"Show me your hands!" he said as he waved his own gloves in the air.

She shook her head no.

Anderson pulled himself higher in his hatch. As he looked down, he noticed that her feet were size 10 or 11, far bigger than any Iraqi woman he had ever seen. *Iraqi women always wear comfortable shoes; sandals or some sort of girl shoes.* He motioned to her again.

Just show me your hands. Again, the tall Iraqi woman shook her head. She began to walk away.

Anderson assessed what he had learned in the last few moments: A tall woman, skinnier than usual, not wearing the right shoes, big feet, and right in the middle of hot spot. She wouldn't reveal her hands.

This is a man. I am 99.9 percent sure this is a man.

As she walked away, Anderson noticed something even more alarming.

The woman, whom he now believed to be a man, was carrying something between her legs.

He has a round strapped between his legs! I can't see it, but just by the way it looks . . . .

Anderson raised his M4 and fired a round into the "woman's" back. The figure collapse into a pile of white fabric. Anderson stood there, his weapon still trained on the pile, as the blast of his rifle echoed through the streets.

Then he questioned himself.

Did I just kill a woman? Did I just kill a woman carrying a kid?

He had to know the answer. Anderson called EOD to clear the body.

While he waited, he and his platoon detained a suspected triggerman, who had exited the same car as the woman. It seemed like it was taking forever for EOD to arrive. The wait provided a grueling period to reflect on what had just happened.

Anderson needed to comfort himself and his men.

"Hey guys, we did the right thing," he said. The men agreed.

155

I know what I saw. I've seen guys carrying rounds before. It's just something I've come to recognize.

EOD arrived in about half an hour and began to work. When the EOD team carefully positioned the body for a search, the veil fell to the ground. Anderson saw a goatee and a red bandana—it was definitely a man.

"Thank God." Relief flooded over him.

Moving the body revealed that the man had been carrying a 120mm shell that was intended to be an IED. The dead man dressed as a woman turned out to be the brother of one of the highest-valued targets in the area.

Lieutenant Anderson climbed back on his tank and continued patrolling north on Route Tampa, noting that he still considered the area around Checkpoint 101 a hot spot.

82. JIM FREEZE

Hello all,

Things have been going really well for me and my platoon, despite the cold, wet weather we've been having. I don't get to watch the news all that often, but when I do, I've noticed that Iraq has not been making the headlines like it was when I first deployed last spring/summer. So while it's not in the news as often as it once was, the reality that our military is at war in a foreign country is still very much a reality to me and the members of my platoon. It seems that the lack of coverage is a good thing because prior to the surge, there were scores of Soldiers dying for seemingly no reason.

Even when I arrived in Iraq, I still struggled with believing whether or not the U.S. should still be here. On the 4th of July last year, I remember having a conversation over some sparkling cider and a cigar with my good friend Austin, and we talked about how if we had to characterize this country in one word, it would be "hopeless." We felt as though that sentiment was echoed throughout America, almost as if the population longed for us to fail and pull out as soon as possible.

It's exciting to me that, now, if I had to characterize Iraq in one word, it would be "progress."

While the progress is not making the news as much as deaths of Service Members once were, I am witnessing it first hand in my everyday work, and I must say it's encouraging.

83. TOMMY BRAMANTI

Two Civil Affairs officers came into Lieutenant Tommy Bramanti's small, cramped office, and gave him a curious look.

"Here you go," said the taller of the two. He presented a thick manila folder from under his shoulder and dropped it on Bramanti's desk. There was a brief pause, and Bramanti endured the awkward silence. *An explanation would be appropriate right about now.*

The shorter of the two chimed in.

"Oh, no one told you?" he asked.

Bramanti pinched his eyebrows together, feigning surprise over his exhaustion.

"You see, this is all the paperwork for the 'Trash for Cash' program . . . and, we," the shorter one said as he motioned to his partner, "have to go. So the program is yours."

Bramanti sensed an upcoming burden despite the comedic scene.

"Long story short, you need to get $50,000 to fund it by next month," said the taller, as the shorter man nodded approvingly.

Bramanti opened the folder and flipped through the stack of paperwork.

"You mean I'm supposed to get funding for your program, and run route-clearance missions at the same time?"

Bramanti's question went unanswered, as the Civil Affairs personnel had already left his office.

A few weeks later, Bramanti was sitting in his Humvee, supervising Day 10 of the "Trash for Cash" program. Iraqi cars, laden with trash they had collected along the street, rolled to the collection point. An Iraqi manager paid for each bag. Bramanti noticed how quickly the streets got cleaner with a little incentive. He exited his Humvee with his interpreter and made small talk with locals returning from the drop-off point.

Bramanti noticed one Iraqi in particular looking back and forth from his newly acquired coins to the interpreter. Spy-like, the local looked to his left and right. He approached Bramanti and began to speak to him in hushed Arabic.

"He says that he's seen al-Qaeda placing IEDs on a road near here," said Tommy's interpreter.

The lieutenant pulled out his map, and the Iraqi pointed to where he'd seen the IEDs.

"Thank you very much," Bramanti responded, and the interpreter translated.

Sure enough, the next day on route clearance, Bramanti's platoon spotted and safely destroyed the disclosed IEDs—thanks to a little intel someone decided to throw out with the trash.

84. BRIAN LEBIEDNIK

Lieutenant Brian Lebiednik and his platoon sergeant realized the enemy had been tracking their platoon. The enemy had followed their movement from cache to cache—until the time had been just right to strike. Even then, the insurgents came out dead.

Still, in continuing the AAR, Lebiednik and his platoon sergeant had realized the enemy had been watching them.

"Sir, what if we used ourselves as bait?" his platoon sergeant asked.

Something about the question just seemed wrong—but the platoon sergeant was definitely onto something.

Why don't we watch them watch us? Just some sort of a distraction to get them moving.

They called it the "Shiny Sparkly."

Their plan was to detonate a safe little explosion in an open area, create some confusion, make the enemy think there's a fight, and watch them flock to the action.

The next time out, Lebiednik's men created a "Shiny Sparkly" just as they'd rehearsed. And as hoped, the enemy used its walkie-talkies, cell phones, and runners to move death squads and snipers in for the kill.

Within a few hours of executing the "Shiny Sparkly," Lebiednik stood watching his platoon methodically search and dismantle an al-Qaeda hideout, where they found two VBIEDs. It felt good to be back in the hunt.

MONTH TWELVE

85. BRAD MELLINGER

Lieutenant Brad Mellinger repeated Jesus's words in his mind.

"Watch and pray."

Even in a scout/sniper hide site in Iraq, Mellinger drew upon his faith. Sometimes he tried to imagine the Garden of Gethsemane, where Jesus had asked his inner circle of disciples to wait nearby . . . .

"Watch and pray."

That's what Mellinger did. And he believed the enemy would come.

The building just through those trees and reeds, near the Tigris River, would draw them back. With patience, Mellinger's men would have their enemy delivered.

Mellinger's men in another position detained two men riding motorcycles along the narrow dirt paths around the building—they had four cell phones between them, and the phones started ringing like crazy. One of the men had $5,000 on him. None of their stories matched up.

The platoon pulled the bikes and the men into their hide site and waited. Within minutes, two more bikers came along, weaving through the trails. Mellinger's Soldiers detained that pair as well.

As the sun was rising, two children came walking up the road to the building. The kids started looking around and milling around the building. The children ran back up the road.

Then, 10 minutes later, two young men approached the building and went inside.

The building had already been declared hostile by Mellinger's Higher. Mellinger moved his platoon into an ambush position just outside the building. He told his men they were clear to engage when the men exited.

The two insurgents came out of the building carrying some bags and boxes. They saw the platoon and began running. The platoon opened fire, killing one of the insurgents, but the other escaped.

AK-47 fire rang out from the platoon's rear, near the main road. The platoon couldn't pursue the enemy without compromising their own security.

Mellinger's men cleared the dead insurgent.

They held on to the four detainees—the motorcycle scouts—for most of the day in their patrol base. After several hours, the platoon moved out of the patrol base and displaced to another position to prepare to fly away. Just prior to final exfil on the aircraft, Mellinger got word that the land-owning unit didn't want to keep the detainees.

Mellinger was angry. He walked up to the detainees, who were still laid out, prepared for exfiltration. He told them they were going to be released.

"You need to understand something," Mellinger said. "If you're gonna keep on doing what you're doing, you're eventually gonna be killed. This is your one opportunity to stand up for your country, to stand up for your children, to stand up for yourself, to stand up for your God. This is a decision that's gonna affect your life. You're either gonna continue to work with terrorists and get killed, or you're gonna change your ways for good and live."

Mellinger hoped that his words and their experience of almost being taken away to a detention facility would influence the men.

Mellinger thought about what to do with the $5,000 his Soldiers had seized from the detainee. He knew he could do anything he wanted with it. He could give it to local Iraqis who really needed it, or he could return it to the detainee.

Brad gave the money back to the detainee.

"Here you go," he said. "You can spend this money however you want. You can buy a bomb, or you can help your family out. But if you choose to buy a bomb, you're gonna die sooner or later."

86. PATRICK HENSON

Lieutenant Pat Henson patrolled on foot with his platoon through the Iraqi neighborhood. They were there to collect atmospherics in their AO, as always, and in particular to find information for a potential mission. Intelligence reported that a leader of sectarian violence had moved into the area. Henson needed to find out where the man was living and then identify a vacant house to use as a staging area on the mission to seize the man.

As he walked along the sidewalk in the darkness of a warm evening, Henson noticed a man waving at him with a huge smile. It was the baker from the bread shop that Henson and his platoon visited several times a week. The bakery was located in a market that was near an Iraqi Police station. Because Henson insisted on conducting joint Iraqi-American patrols every other day, and since the Iraqis did not like to walk far, Henson had spent a lot of time on patrol in that market. He and his Soldiers regularly stopped to buy bread and to talk with the baker. They had even baked their own bread there on several occasions.

The baker greeted Henson with a hug and invited him into his home for *chai*. The patrol stopped to pull security outside as Pat and his platoon sergeant removed their helmets, took a seat in the living room, enjoyed hot sweetened tea, and visited with their friend.

After a few minutes of small talk, the baker began expressing his concerns about recent changes in his neighborhood.

"There is trouble in my neighborhood," he lamented. "New people, bad people, moved in three houses down, in Number Five. They have forced some of my long-time friends to leave their homes. The family in the house right next to them, four houses down, left yesterday, afraid for their lives. This is awful, awful for Iraq."

Henson couldn't believe his good luck. Without realizing it, the baker had just provided him the information he sought—the location of the HVI, as well a vacant house from which to recon the target and stage the mission.

87. CLINT SPEEGLE

Lieutenant Clint Speegle could hear the conversation with his JAG in his head, even as he was flying back to Taji in his Apache.

"You know you could've shot," the JAG would surely say.

Speegle knew the ROE, but he had made a moral judgment and saved his bullets. He knew those men were as good as dead, but he didn't want to be the one to kill them.

As always, he'd sit down with the JAG and go over his gun tapes, a task he takes as no less important than the hours he spends helping the crew chiefs take oil samples and inspect the helicopter. He'd roll up his sleeves and look over their shoulders, asking questions about the airframe and their actions to keep the aircraft in good condition. He did the same here for his mind.

His wingman and he had been out trolling the AO, looking for something to do on an uneventful day. They decided to track the Division boundary, out in the open desert. They flew upon a small hut with a truck nearby in the middle of nowhere.

Speegle had no communications with the local ground unit, no communications with his own battalion, and "splotchy" communications with Air Traffic Control. He wanted to get out of there so he could talk to somebody.

When he looked more closely at the hut and truck, however, he noticed four men on their knees, hands bound behind their backs. He saw three or four other men with AK-47s who were on their knees praying. As soon as the Apaches neared, the men tried to hide their weapons but remained close to the hostages.

It appeared to the aviators that they'd happened upon an imminent execution. Speegle started debating with his back-seater about what to do.

"We're running out of gas," Speegle said. "The guys that are tied up are dead any way you look at it. If we engage, we kill the three or four bad guys, but we also kill these guys that are tied up."

Do I need to pull the trigger on these guys or do I not pull the trigger?

The armed men stood their ground, took their chances, and waited for the Apaches to leave. Speegle and his wingman eventually ran low on fuel. For Speegle, he couldn't live with killing four innocent civilians. And so he flew away.

88. DAN BARINGER

Dan Baringer sat at a meal meeting where many of the local leaders had gathered. They were all celebrating the progress they'd made by working together.

The money had been flowing well in the last few months, and there had been a significant decrease in IEDs. Still, some of Dan's Soldiers questioned why they were paying the locals more than most of the platoon in order to control the IEDs. The rationale for Dan was easy: *I'll pay the money all day long if it means my Soldiers all come home alive.*

Yet, as Dan looked around the room at the gathering of men enjoying a lavish meal and good company, he realized that he'd previously met at least a handful of his new Iraqi friends. He had detained them when they were his enemies just a few short months ago.

89. JIM FREEZE

We passed the one-year mark at the beginning of this month. It's been a long, hard journey, that's for sure. The weather is changing, bringing back the memories of what things were like when we first arrived. The inexperience we had when we showed up is long gone; we now travel our areas like celebrities or dignitaries. We've helped make such a positive difference here at the local level it's almost unbelievable, even though I witness it every day. I don't think I have even begun to absorb it all in my mind, but I'm beginning to see it as we prepare to hand over the area to the next unit.

As a result, local governments are functioning and are receiving money from the province. Businesses are up and running. Iraqi Army units are securing their areas on their own and conducting missions with no help from the U.S.

Police forces are patrolling the streets and investigating crimes. Distribution of food and fuel is functioning and citizens are getting their monthly rations. Schools are educating thousands more children than when we first arrived. Clinics are operating with regular hours. Families are receiving reparations payments from the government and rebuilding their battle-damaged homes. Men from tribes are sitting together and talking about their issues instead of shooting one another and planting bombs in their roads. People are receiving financial aid from the government to help them rebuild businesses and livelihood. Farms are producing and selling goods in the market. Water is flowing in the canals despite the drought. Electricity is at the best it's been since 2003. And at the forefront, people all across the region feel safe. They agree that security has improved dramatically, and after living in fear for so long, security is more important than any of the other improvements.

Doing all this work, day in and day out, with only a two-week break eight months ago . . . I'm tired. I've personally experienced the horrors of having a brother killed by destructive factions and another sent home with a gunshot wound that shattered his arm, and I've also known how exhausting it is just to be away from the comforts of the great U.S. of A for such a long time. I'm very ready to be at home, relaxing and not worrying about the entire well-being of not only my platoon—the best platoon a guy could ask for—but of tens of thousands of Iraqi citizens in eight villages that we labored and toiled in (with? for?) over the last 12 months.

No doubt, I will remember the men I spent every day alongside, struggling through all of this, and I will also remember the Iraqis who've chosen to take a stand against the insurgents and militias and make Iraq a better place for their children. I'm so proud of the work my platoon has accomplished since being over here, and I'm proud of the brave citizens of Iraq for their struggles as well. I can only pray that our work will not be for naught as we prepare to leave and that our efforts will bring to fruition more successes that will firmly establish Iraq as a successful, sovereign nation. And that as a result, we can bring the troops home in victory.

90. JOHN MAURO

Lieutenant John Mauro had volunteered to accompany the combat logistics patrol. This would be his final patrol in Iraq . . . at least on this deployment. As he sat in the front right seat of the Humvee gun truck that had carried him safely across hundreds of miles of Iraq over the past year, John felt emotionally connected to it. Now, though, it was no longer "his" truck. It had been signed over to the incoming unit.

Across from him, driving the gun truck, was the patrol leader, a young-looking staff sergeant from the incoming unit. Her convoy was delivering Class I, II, IV, and IX to a smaller FOB.

"Alpha Three-Four, this is Three-Three," squawked an urgent voice over the radio. "Your truck is smoking."

"Oh, my God. What do we do?" the patrol leader asked Mauro.

"Stop the truck," he told her, and she did.

John exited the truck immediately, as did the gunner and the Soldiers in the back seats. Once outside, he could see that the front right tire had caught on fire. He yelled and motioned for fire extinguishers. Then he noticed that the patrol leader was still in the driver's seat.

Mauro walked around the front of the truck, motioning with his arm for her to exit. She remained in her seat, still gripping the steering wheel. Mauro opened her door.

"Get the hell out of the vehicle!" he said.

"Dismount?" she asked. "Is it safe?"

"It's a lot safer out here than it is in a burning truck," the experienced PL replied. Mauro had spent weeks in this neighborhood. He knew it was relatively safe. Plus, the patrol was within sight of an IP check point.

The patrol leader finally stepped out of the truck and stood next to Mauro, watching Soldiers put out the flames with fire extinguishers.

"You're the patrol leader," John quietly reminded her.

Still, she stood there. John realized that he needed to do some coaching.

"Your Soldiers are looking to you for information and guidance," he advised. "Get on the net and tell everyone what's going on, and then direct your trucks to establish security for the recovery operation."

She made the radio calls and returned to Mauro.

"What else do you need to be doing?" he prompted her.

"Call back to have a recovery vehicle sent here?" she asked.

"Well, what assets do you already have with you?"

This prompted her to recall that the convoy already included a wrecker.

With Mauro's continued coaching, the patrol leader managed to direct the vehicle's recovery and to complete the patrol.

At the conclusion of his final patrol, Mauro stared at his former truck, his beloved "A3." John's unit had taken care of that truck for a year and it had run like a stallion, yet in less than a week the incoming unit had destroyed it. He hoped that this incident wasn't a sign of things to come. He and his Soldiers had worked too hard and sacrificed too much.

91. BRETT KRONICK

The mood was jubilant as Lieutenant Brett Kronick approached his Soldiers to conduct the patrol brief. The platoon had successfully executed more than 180 patrols as their Task-Force Assault-CP's PSD. Against all odds, they were about to complete their deployment without having suffered any serious casualties. This would be their final mission "outside the wire."

Kronick never cut corners when it came to PCCs and patrol briefs. With his Soldiers gathered around him, he took accountability and got a thumbs up from each truck on radio checks.

As he had so many times, Kronick gave his Soldiers their task and purpose. This time, it felt great.

"Our task today is to transport Justice Six safely to Camp Victory," he said. "Our purpose is so we can all go home!"

His Soldiers whooped it up.

Kronick announced the route—one they all knew to be safe—the order of movement, and recent intel update. He asked if anyone had any observations to add about the route or SITREP. There were none this time.

As per SOP, Kronick led talk-through rehearsals of actions on SAF, actions on IED, CASEVAC, actions on breakdown, actions on a vehicle fire, actions on rollover, and EOF procedures. For each topic, he selected one Soldier to explain aloud the unit's SOP. Every Soldier knew it all by heart. They were ready to roll for one last time.

"Load up," Kronick ordered, and his Soldiers moved into their vehicles with a lightness he'd never seen.

As the patrol exited the ECP, the chatter on the net was about German beer. This prompted Kronick to think about his next leadership challenge—keeping his guys from stupidly killing themselves at home after bravely surviving a year of war.

"There's a cordon up ahead," reported the lead vehicle.

The convoy slowed but kept moving.

Kronick's truck passed a Stryker that had established a cordon along the highway. Its Soldiers looked angry. A minute later, he passed the reason for the cordon. A Stryker had been destroyed by an EFP. There were casualties.

Kronick didn't say anything over the net. He didn't have to. He could sense that his Soldiers, like himself, had refocused on the mission at hand. *It's not over till it's over.* There was no more idle chatter.

After arriving at their destination, the platoon halted to clear their weapons. The *chink-chink-chink* of bolts riding forward sounded like the bells of a celebration. Now, at last, it really was over.

HOME

92. SCHUYLER WILLIAMSON

Lieutenant Schuyler Williamson gazed out the bus window at the passing lights of Fort Hood. It was hard to believe that he was finally back in America. Everything looked so strangely peaceful and routine. He felt a slight tremor inside and wondered whether it was caused by exhaustion or excitement.

The convoy of busses came to a stop at the Division parade field. To his left, under the lights across the field, Schuyler could see the crowd of family members and friends who awaited his battalion. He knew that his was somewhere in that crowd, and his parents, too.

He filed off the bus with his Soldiers. He and the rest of the battalion from the other busses formed up into a formation in the street, where the line of busses blocked them from view of their families. The night air was cool and smelled like home.

A chant from across the field started softly and grew progressively louder and louder.

"Move that bus! Move that bus! Move that bus!"

It reminded Williamson of the television show *Extreme Home Makeover.*

As soon as the unit was formed, the busses drove away, and to the wild cheers of the crowd Williamson marched forward among the Soldiers of the platoon, the company, and the battalion that he had experienced a year of war with. The formation halted in the middle of the parade field. A senior officer from the Division spoke some words welcoming them home. Williamson's eyes scanned the crowd for his family, to no avail.

The senior officer's brief comments ended with, "Families and loved ones, go get your Soldier!"

With a roar, the crowd of loved ones surged forward, merging into the formation of Soldiers. It was chaos-hugs, smiles, tears, people everywhere. Williamson kept looking through the crowd, but he could not find his family.

"Schuyler!" It was his father's familiar voice.

Williamson turned to see his dad moving toward him. Then he saw *her*. Rushing past his dad, moving as quickly as she could through the crowd towards Williamson, was Kristen, his wife. She collapsed into his arms, a year's worth of worry and loneliness flowing out in her tears. After a long embrace, Williamson reunited with his parents. They looked as happy as he had ever seen them.

Then he felt a tap on his shoulder from behind. It was from one of his Soldiers.

"Sir," said his Soldier. "I really want you to meet my dad. He doesn't speak English. But I really want you to meet him."

Williamson stretched out his hand to the man. The Soldier's dad squeezed the lieutenant's arm with a firm two-handed handshake. He looked directly into the eyes of his son's platoon leader, offering a wordless expression of gratitude for bringing his son home alive, breaking into tears as his son spoke.

"Sir," said the Soldier to his platoon leader, "I just want you to know, I will fight with you anytime, anywhere."

Watching all this, Kristen finally understood why her husband was so committed to serving his Soldiers. He was their platoon leader.

LIST OF STORIES

Prologue: Adam Herndon (bus sniper?)

1. Matt Martinez (deployment order)
2. Jim Freeze email (arrival in country)
3. Greg Cartier (new unit and mission)
4. Jim Freeze email (beginning mission)
5. Mike Valentine (RIP/TOA)
6. Mike Faber (ham joke in DFAC)
7. Stephanie Gillespie (patrol uniform)
8. Brian Lebiednik (weapons in home)
9. Ben Weakley (building barriers)
10. Clint Speegle (first contact)
11. Kevin Stein (low-speed chase)
12. Karl Simpkins* (hateful to locals)
13. Dave MacPhail (EFP on MRAP)
14. Chris Defiori (sensing session)
15. Joe Tomasello (IED overwatch-blue)
16. Chris Larsen (IED overwatch-youth)
17. Megan Williams (white lie)
18. Craig Arnold (baited ambush)
19. Curtis Minor (cache/rug casevac)
20. Dan Riordan (Hollywood PSG)
21. Jim Guggenheim (JDAM strike)
22. Mike Rash (blown from truck)
23. Ryan Harbick (re-looking a mission)
24. Jon Sherrill (sniper attack at TCP)
25. Mike Steele (donkey in road)
26. Trevor Buckey* (ND)
27. Brian Larson (no-wire TCP)
28. Chris Ford (mosque-monitor family)
29. Bryan Crossman (mosque-armed kids)
30. Casey Baker (PSG-SL dispute)
31. Mark Hien* (stops a beating)

32. John Rogers (HETs ambushed on MSR)
33. Ben Melton (IED built into school)
34. Murphy White* (unsecured .50 cal)
35. Stephen DuPerre (mistaken PID)
36. Jim Freeze (support from home)
37. Brian Larson (hesitation to shoot)
38. Jared Oren (stolen wood)
39. Brittany Meeks (secure crash site)
40. Doug Boldwin* (TQ, unwritten rules)
41. Chris Crofford (reporting abuse)
42. Chris Ford (NP standoff)
43. Gavin Hadduck* (no more nice)
44. John Dolan (gunboat firefight)
45. Matt Martinez (carjack victim)
46. Patrick Henson (family cell phones)
47. Schuyler Williamson (joins a fight)
48. Derek Syed (shot by sniper)
49. Zack Cooley* ('key' payback)
50. Laura Weimer (new PL doubts)
51. Shawn Jokinen (VBIED)
52. Matt Burch (response to VBIED)
53. Steve LeDroiux* (play-acting TQ)
54. Elizabeth Zerwick (meal of honor)
55. Jed Pomfret* (accepting the deal)
56. Jesse Allgeyer (tip line)
57. Mike Johnston (the 'rat claw')
58. Kai Hawkins (calm voice on net)
59. Donnie Suchane* (fear after IED)
60. Shawn Jokinen (counter-IED SKT)
61. Herman Bulls (shared sacrifice)
62. Tom Hickey (saving a girl)
63. Jim Freeze email (what war is)
64. Isaac Widnasz* (lost composure)
65. Matt Martinez (catastrophic IED)
66. Vicki Tappra* (possible IED)
67. Jason Koslovsky* (suicidal Soldier)
68. Brad Mellinger (ambushing AQI)
69. Jared Oren (stealing parts)

* Indicates that the name provided in the story is not the actual platoon leader's name.

An index for this book is available online at http://proreading. army.mil, which is the professional reading and discussion forum within MilSpace.

MilSpace also includes the Army's professional forums of:

Company Commanders, http://CC.army.mil & Platoon Leaders, http://PL.army.mil

If you are a currently commissioned officer who is a past, present, or future CC or PL, join your forum and become more effective.

Interview/Research team: LTC Pete Kilner, LTC Nate Allen, & Nate Self.

Writing and editing team: LTC Pete Kilner & Nate Self

Send your feedback to PL.Team@us.army.mil

ACKNOWLEDGEMENTS

Props and thanks to all the great people who contributed to shaping this book:

Nate Allen, Steve Aude, Kevin Badger, Dave Bair, Josh Bookout, Todd Brown, J.B. Burton, John Bryan, Tony Burgess, Jon Campbell, Pat Campbell, Bob Caslen, Katie Christy, Rich Chudzik, Brent Clemmer, Kevin Cutright, Denise Corbari, Chris Danbeck, Rob Dees, Chris Douglas, Jon Dunn, Ryan Ebel, Bob Eichenger, Brit Erslev, Joe Ewers, Mark Federovich, Patrick Finnegan, Paul Funk, Jamey Gadoury, Sena Garven, Gian Gentile, Joe Geraci, Luke Gilliam, Penny Glackin, Vicki Goble, Lisa Griffin, Rob Griggs, George Hallenbeck, Matt Hardman, Brett Hersley, Ed House, Mike Infante, Chris Kayes, Pete Kilner, Ray Kimball, Brian Koyn, Ryan Kranc, Paul Krattiger, Joe LeBouef, Gus Lee, Vince Lindenmeyer, Anthony Lupo, Brett Martin, Neal Mayo, Patrick Michaelis, Chris Miller, Steve Miska, Tom Morel, Dave Oclander, Mike O'Meara, Joe Psotka, Dan Ragsdale, Casey Randall, Cheryl Rau, Guy Rogers III, Kim Rowe, Nicole Scott, Nate Self, Mike Shekleton, Jon Silk, Tom Spahr, Terese Sweet, Scott Todd, Kevin Toner, Steve Townsend, Mark Tribus, Jeff Van Antwerp, Al Vigilante, Tyson Voelkel, Jared Wilson, Adam Wojcik, Ryan Wylie.

A GLOSSARY OF ACRONYMS

AAR:	After Action Review
ACOG:	Advanced Combat Optical Gunsight
ACU:	Advanced Combat Uniform
A-10:	Thunderbolt II, single-seat, twin-engine jet aircraft that provides close air support (CAS)
AH-64:	Twin engine, four-bladed attack helicopter
AIF:	Anti-Iraqi Forces
AK-47:	automatic weapon that fires 7.62mm
AO:	Area of Operations
A/S-3:	Assistant Operations Officer
AQI:	al-Qaeda in Iraq
AWT:	Air Weapons Team
BBC:	British Broadcasting Corporation
BHA:	Brigade Holding Area
Black list:	list of persons to detain
BP:	Battle Position
BC:	Battalion Commander, Battery Commander, or Bradley Commander
BFT:	Blue Force Tracker
BFV:	Bradley Fighting Vehicle
BSTB:	Brigade Special Troops Battalion
CAB:	Combat Action Badge
CASEVAC:	Casualty evacuation by ground
CIF:	Central Issue Facility
CSH:	Combat Support Hospital
CLP:	Combat Logistics Patrol
CLS:	Combat Lifesaver
CO:	Commanding officer
Comms:	Communications
COP:	Combat Outpost
CP:	Command Post
DAPs:	Deltoid and Axillary Protector components of the IBA

DFAC: Dining facility
ECP: Entry Control Point
EFP: Explosively-Formed Penetrator
EOD: Explosive Ordnance Disposal
EOF: Escalation of Force
ER: Emergency Room
ESV: Engineer Stryker Vehicle
Exfil: Exfiltration
Five W's: Who, What, When, Where, Why
FLIR: Forward-Looking Infrared Radar
FO: Forward Observer
FOB: Forward Operating Base
FRAGO: Fragmentary Order
HE: High-Explosive
HET: Heavy Equipment Transporter
HUMINT: Human Intelligence
HVI/T: High-Value Individual/Target
IBA: Interceptor Body Armor
IED: Improvised Explosive Device
Infil: Infiltration
Info: Information
Intel: Intelligence
IO: Information Operations
IP: Iraqi Police
ISR: Intelligence, Surveillance, and Reconnaissance
IZ: International (Green) Zone
JAG: Judge Advocate General
JAM: Jaysh al-Mahdi, a.k.a. Mahdi Militia, paramilitary force
               of Iraqi Shiite cleric Muqtada al-Sadr
JDAM: Joint Direct Attack Munition
J-Lens: A high-power optical site, usually mounted on a tower
               at COPs to observe the surrounding area.
LZ: Landing Zone
MBITR: Multi-Band Intra-Team Radio
MEDEVAC: Medical Evacuation by Aircraft
Mk19:   Belt-fed automatic, 40mm grenade launcher
MP: Military Police
MSR: Main Supply Route

MRAP:	Mine-Resistant Ambush-Protected vehicle
M1A2:	Abrams Main Battle Tank
M2:	Browning .50 Caliber machine gun
M203:	Single shot 40mm grenade launcher frequently attached to M4
M240:	Belt-fed machine gun, fires 7.62mm round
M249:	Squad Automatic Weapon, fires a 5.56mm round
M4:	Shorter and lighter version of M16 carbine
M9:	9mm pistol
NCO:	Non-Commissioned Officer
ND:	Negligent Discharge
NP:	National Police
NVG:	Night Vision Goggles
OP:	Observation Post
OPTEMPO:	Operational Tempo
PA:	Physician's Assistant
PCC/PCI:	Pre-Combat Checks/Pre-Combat Inspections
PID:	Positive Identification
PK or PKC:	Russian Acroynym for "Kalashnikov's Machine Gun"
PFC:	Private First Class
PL:	Platoon Leader
PLS:	Palletized Load System
POO:	Point of Origin
PSD:	Personal Security Detachment
PSG:	Platoon Sergeant
PSYOP:	Psychological Operations
PT:	Physical Training
PTSD:	Post-Traumatic Stress Disorder
QRF:	Quick Reaction Force
RIP/TOA:	Relief in Place/Transition of Authority
ROE:	Rules of Engagement
RPG:	Rocket-Propelled Grenade
RTD:	Returned to Duty
RTO:	Radio Telephone Operator
SAF:	Small-Arms Fire
SAPI:	Small-Arms Protective Inserts
SAW:	Squad Automatic Weapon
SCO:	Squadron Commander

SIGINT:	Signals Intelligence
SITREP:	Situation Report
SKEDCO:	Brand of collapsible litter
SKS:	"Samozaryadniy Karabin Sistemi Simonova," Russian translation of "Self-loading Carbine, Simonov's System"
SOP:	Standing Operating Procedure
SP:	Start Point
Stryker:	Eight-wheeled armored vehicle
SUV:	Sport Utility Vehicle
S-2:	Intelligence Officer
S-3:	Operations Officer
SVBIED:	Suicide Vehicle-borne Improvised Explosive Device
TAC:	Tactical Command Post
TC:	Truck Commander or Tank Commander
TCP:	Traffic Control Point
Terp:	Interpreter
TOA:	Transfer of Authority
TOC:	Tactical Operations Center
Transpo:	Transportion
TTP:	Tactic, Technique, and Procedure
UAV:	Unmanned Aerial Vehicle
UCMJ:	Uniform Code of Military Justice
UXO:	Unexploded Ordnance
VBIED:	Vehicle-Borne Improvised Explosive Device
XO:	Executive officer
9-Line:	MEDEVAC request format, contains nine lines of data
15-6:	an official Army investigation
19K:	Armor Crewman
.50 Cal:	M2 Browning .50 Caliber Machine Gun

INDEX

These themes can be found using the following story numbers.